SUOMALAISEN TIEDEAKATEMIAN TOIMITUKSIA
HUMANIORA 330
ANNALES ACADEMIÆ SCIENTIARUM FENNICÆ

DAGHESTAN AND

THE WORLD OF ISLAM

EDITED BY

MOSHE GAMMER AND DAVID J. WASSERSTEIN

DAGHESTAN AND THE WORLD OF ISLAM

Annales Academiæ Scientiarum Fennicæ is part of the publishing co-operation between the Finnish Academy of Science and Letters and the Finnish Society of Science and Letters.

The series Humaniora continues the former ser. B.

Editor:
Professor Heikki Palva
Viheriötie 5
04310 Tuusula
Finland

Associate editor:
Kaj Öhrnberg
Merikasarminkatu 10 B 43
00160 Helsinki
Finland

Cover:
Juha Markula

Distributor
Bookstore Tiedekirja
Kirkkokatu 14, 00170 Helsinki
Finland
Tel. +358-9-635 177
Fax + 358-9-635 017
Email: tiedekirja@tsv.fi

ISSN: 1239-6982
ISBN: 951-41-0945-7

Printed by Gummerus Kirjapaino Oy, Vaajakoski 2006

CONTENTS

Moshe Gammer and David J. Wasserstein

Preface

7

Harun Ibrahimov

Daghestan and the Near East before Islam

11

Vladimir Bobrovnikov

Abu Muslim in Islamic History and Mythology of the

Northern Caucasus

23

Amri Shikhsaidov

The Political History of Daghestan in

the Tenth–Fifteenth Centuries

45

Moshe Gammer

The Introduction of the Khalidiyya and the Qadiriyya into

Daghestan in the Nineteenth Century

55

Butrus Abu-Manneh

The Role of Shaykh Isma'il al-Shirwani in

the Khalidi Sub-Order

69

SONIA CHESNIN

Hasan al-Alqadari

The Last Representative of Traditional

Learning in Daghestan

81

MICHAEL KEMPER

Daghestani Shaykhs and Scholars in Russian Exile:

Networks of Sufism, *Fatwas* and Poetry

95

HELMA VAN DEN BERG

A Darghi Codex of Customary Law and its

Contribution to Linguistics

109

PREFACE

The papers collected in this volume were all presented in their original forms at a meeting in Tel Aviv University in February 2001, dedicated to the subject of 'Daghestan in the World of Islam'. Participants came from within Israel itself, from Daghestan, from Germany, from Russia and from Holland, attesting to the broad and international, if still insufficiently dense, nature of scholarly interest in Daghestan.

The initial impetus for the meeting which led to the production of this volume derives from a project, supported by INTAS, the International Association for the Promotion of Co-operation with Scientists from the New Independent States (NIS) of the Former Soviet Union, which we began in 2000. The central concern of the project is with the "location, identification, retrieval, recording and publication of oriental manuscript resources in Daghestan as a preliminary to major scholarly study of the Islamic history of the region". It became clear to us, at a very early stage of our work, both that one important by-product of this project was the scholarly contacts which it made possible between ourselves and colleagues in Daghestan and elsewhere and that there is a great dearth of publication on Caucasian Islam in western languages (where western means both western in relation to the languages of Islam and western in relation to the languages of eastern Europe and the Caucasus). The opportunity thus offered seemed too good to lose, and we seized the possibility of holding, on the margins of our larger project, what we hope will be the first of a series of meetings on subjects devoted to Daghestani, and more broadly Caucasian, Islamic subjects.

The project itself was an attempt to co-operate with colleagues in Daghestan in the identification of collections of manuscripts of oriental interest, in all languages and in all scripts, and in starting to prepare catalogues to western standards and in western styles, for use by colleagues in Daghestan and outside. Our project is in one sense an experiment or a trailblazer, for little if anything has been done so far to make the existence, far less the contents, of such collections properly known in the west. We cannot hope to do more than scratch the surface, both because there are numerous collections, public and private, in Daghestan and because the task of cataloguing them is complex and beset with difficulties deriving in part from local conditions. In addition, the project suffered from delays imposed by the security situation both in Daghestan itself and in Israel. Overall, however, the project has proven itself a success: members of the teams from Daghestan visited Israel and worked there with members of the Israeli team, and in Daghestan expeditions were undertaken to various parts of the country in order to identify and to collect information about numerous collections. Already the fruits of this collaboration are beginning to appear and this volume of studies is an earnest example of what is to come.

This first meeting was, perhaps inevitably, general in subject, but as the contents page alone makes abundantly clear, a number of issues of central concern came to the fore in our discussions: first, the importance of al-Ghazali and of Sufism in general for the spread of Islam and the florescence of Islamic culture in the region; second, the diversity of the Islamic experience here, with Daghestan experiencing a very early islamization, and Chechnya, say, becoming islamized at a much later date; third, the richness of the manuscript resources of the area, which have still to be fully explored; this is the central concern of our project; fourth, even taking account of the material available in Arabic and in Russian, far too little is known about the medieval Islamic history of the Caucasus, and we need to have much more by way of research in this field. In part this comes up against the problem of the existence of a large number of languages which are spoken by small numbers of people and which have as yet been little studied, sometimes even little recorded, and one of the papers in this volume is devoted to an early record of one such language from the region. Several of the papers point to the fact that the region was not only Islamic but fully integrated into the cultural world of Islam. Although we have the occasional article on topics like the links between Daghestan and Yemen, we need many more such studies to clarify the ties between Daghestan and more central places like Baghdad. The remarks on such links scattered here and there through these papers show that there is still much to be found, particularly for the medieval and early modern periods. Scholarly interest in the nineteenth and twentieth centuries, and the Russian impact on the area, should not make us forget the earlier periods.

We are grateful for their support, financial, administrative, moral and other, given by INTAS, as well as by the Department of Middle Eastern and African History, the School of History and the Faculty of Humanities at Tel Aviv University, as well as the then heads of these bodies. Our colleagues Heikki Palva and Kaj Öhrnberg made it possible for this volume to appear in the series of the Finnish Academy of Science and Letters, and our thanks go also to them and to the Academy itself. Last, but not least, Dr. Baruch Podolsky of Tel Aviv University was of great help in linguistic transliteration.

While this volume was in preparation, we learned with shock and sadness of the sudden death, while on a research trip in the Caucasus, of one of the contributors to this volume, our colleague and friend Helma van den Berg. Our sympathies go to her husband, Leo Vogelenzang, as well as our thanks for his help in locating and sending to us the text of her paper in this collection. Inevitably, it was not possible for her to give the paper the final revisions which she would have wished to give it, but even in its unpolished state, it constitutes a valuable contribution to the study of one of the smaller languages of the area, and is an indication of the work that was to have been expected of her had she lived. We salute her memory.

Moshe Gammer

David J. Wasserstein

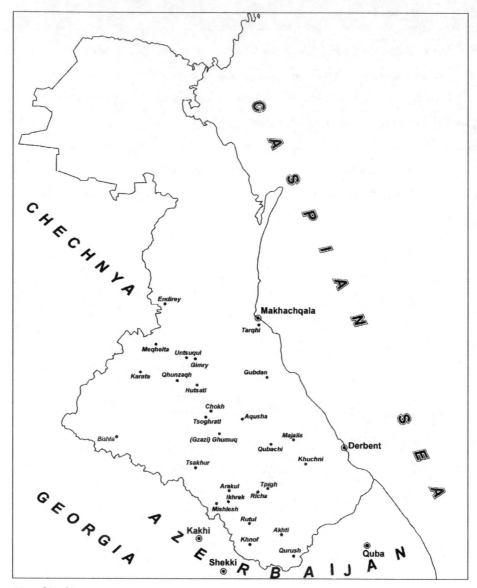

Map of Daghestan.

DAGHESTAN AND THE NEAR EAST
BEFORE ISLAM

HARUN IBRAHIMOV

The term Daghestan has various meanings: there is a distinction between historical – that is pre-Islamic – Daghestan and Islamic Daghestan which came into being after the disintegration of the historical Caucasian Albania (3rd century BCE to 10th century CE). The meaning of the term "Daghestan" (in local languages "Dağıstan") is connected with Turko-Iranian tradition: *dağ* is 'mountain' in Turkic languages, *stan* in Farsi is "locality", "region"; thus the term Daghestan means literally "Mountain Land". It appears at the turn of the tenth century CE, and is to a certain degree a translation of the name "Alban". The structure of "Alban" contains two elements: *al* – with the meaning of "upper" – and *ban* with the meaning of "mountain". Both of these elements retained their primary meaning in the Tsakhur and Rutul languages; for example, in Rutul *ban* – mountain; *bana ru'ura* – "I am going to the mountain" (literally: "in mountain going is"); in Tsakhur *ban-as* "piedmont", *alaqana* – "upper-highlander", *alaqanbi* – "upper-highlanders", "dwellers of the mountains". Many of those who study the history, culture, traditions and socio-political structure of the peoples of Daghestan share the opinion that the toponym "Albania", just like the toponym "Daghestan", means Mountain Land. Therefore the toponyms Caucasian Albania (in some sources historical Caucasian Albania) and Daghestan are equal in their semantics and refer to the same region. In consequence in works on the toponym Albania a more specific definition was added, for clarification: apart from Caucasian Albania there is also Balkan Albania. The meaning Caucasian Albania is fully equal to the term historical Daghestan. Pre-Islamic Daghestan is to a certain extent Caucasian Albania.[1]

The Caucasus was a part of the ancient Near East, and, more than that, it belonged to the culture of the Near East. The Near and Middle East and the Caucasus are one whole. This unity is clearly seen both in such areas as agriculture and early metal technology and in the spiritual sphere. In connection with this we should note that the peoples of the Northern Caucasus and in particular the North-Eastern Caucasus (the Nakh-Daghestani) peoples, are generally reckoned to be the most ancient inhabitants of the region. It is thought that they have lived here for more than ten thousand years. This ancient connection between the peoples of the Caucasus and those of the Middle and Near East is still felt in many important spheres despite the huge time span and the ethno-cultural, socio-political, spiritual, moral and also to a certain degree ecological differences between them. In my view, this unity between the Caucasus and the Near and Middle East is preserved first of all in the human factor: their souls, worldview, and spirit have remained "familial". There still exist a variety of hypotheses concerning the relationship of the Caucasian languages (and in particular of the languages of the North-Eastern Caucasus) with some languages of the Near and Middle East. These concern first of all the languages of the Hittites, of the Proto-Hittites, the most ancient population of Asia Minor, of the Hurrites, of Urartu and others.[2] In this area science still has a long way to go.

The connection of Daghestan and its peoples to the civilisations of the Mediterranean basin, with the first cradles of humanity, is confirmed by the high level of agriculture, specifically the terrace agriculture in the mountains; the artificial irrigation systems; the protection of the environment, first of all land; the culture of small stock grazing, especially sheep, common to the mountains and the lowlands; the preservation of the fertility of the land; and much more. One needs only mention that in the past (and until recently) Daghestan grew almost 60 varieties of wheat, and several dozen kinds of beans, primarily lentils. Many Daghestanis living on the frontier between the mountains and the Kura-Alazan valley were accomplished agriculturists and pastoralists. The grazing of sheep – as opposed to large stock – demanded specialised ways of maintaining the herds. The Tsakhurs in particular were greatly skilled in this profession. Mastery of the mountains by the Tsakhurs and by the other peoples – in particular the Kryz, the Budukh, the Hinalug (that is, peoples living in the upper mountains), and partially by the Kurins (that is Lezgins), Rutuls and others – started at the end of the 3rd-beginning of the 2nd millennium BCE. Mastery of the mountains (that is summer pastures) was connected, first of all, with the development of sheep-raising into an independent, and highly profitable branch of the economy. Evidence of this can be seen in the history of the Tsakhur settlements in the Gal (the Kura-Alazan valley) and the upper Samur *mahal* (in the mountains) which have common (repeating, identical) names: Lek – Lekid – Lek Kutyuklu; Tsakh – Artsakh (< Arantsakh); Mishlesh – Mishlesh; Jinikh – Jinikh; Kalel – Kalel; Mukhakh – Mukhakh. Sometimes explanations were

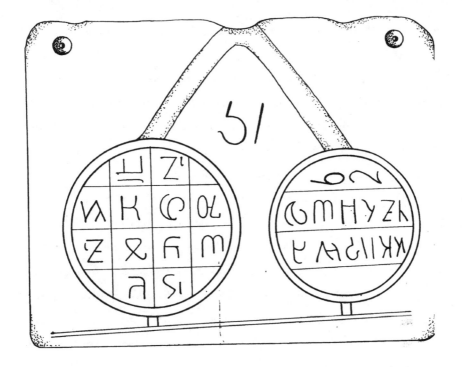

added to these names, like Agdam-Kalel, Bash-Mukhakh. In other, less frequent instances, names of villages were changed, for example Mishlesh > Chinchar (Chīinchlar), Lek > Kurdul, Jinikh > Gullyug etc. The conquest of the high mountains, which proceeded from the lowlands, did not disjoint the economy but rather broadened it. During the Caucasian War in the 19th century many officials of the Tsarist administration visiting mountain villages were amazed at the affluence of the highlanders (here the reference is specifically to the Tsakhurs of Mountain *mahals*) who lacked pasture land at all, or in the best case owned tiny areas. This affluence was secured by the highly developed agriculture in the Kura-Alazan valley (which according to Roman historians and geographers was more fertile than the land of Egypt) as well as by the use of the rich summer pastures in the mountains and the good winter pastures in the lowlands.

It is remarkable that also in material culture there are many similarities between the peoples of Daghestan (and of the Caucasus in general) and those of the eastern Mediterranean, such as types of house, the manner of construction (true, here local climatic, topographic and other conditions were of primary influence), the shape and design of fret tools and sickles, grain graters, the type and form of ceramics, vessels, and sometimes even similarity or closeness in their names.

The pre-Islamic period in Daghestan is also interesting because it was at that time that the ethno-cultural and ethno-linguistic character of Daghestan started to form. Daghestan has experienced a continuous and uninterrupted development of local culture from the 3rd–2nd millennium BCE onward.[3] This is a difficult and complex problem, which has been very little studied. However, one thing is clear: at that time there began the process of autonomisation of the ethno-linguistic regions of Daghestan, or more precisely the Eastern Caucasian languages, into the Nakh and the Daghestani languages. The Nakh linguistic group includes Checheno-Ingush (which from the 18th century divided into the Chechen and Ingush languages) and Batsby (at present its speakers live within the republic of Georgia, are Christians and described in their internal passports as Georgians). The Daghestani group of languages consists of 26 languages and is divided into three genetically close groups: first, the Avar-Andi-Tsez group (at the moment this includes 14 languages: the Avar language, 8 Andi languages, and 5 Tsez languages); secondly, the Darghi-Lak group (because of the neutralisation of Darghi and the large number of strongly different dialects, some of the members of this group are considered by specialists as independent languages, for example, Kubachi, Megheb, Qaitagh); and thirdly, the Samur or Lezgin group with its ten languages. These are divided according to their genetic closeness into the eastern and western sub-groups, while three languages (Archi, Udi and Khinalug) are so far removed by their structural-system characteristics that some scholars see in them wholly distinct languages, not belonging to this group. The processes of language development (differentiation, integration, regional coalition etc.) are not always straightforward. Irregularities, local specificities and non-standard developments can always be found. All that can be said for sure at the moment is that by the time of Daghestan's islamization the ethno-linguistic and ethno-cultural character of the region was already formed.

This phenomenon was important for historical Daghestan, facilitating the formation of ethnic consciousness. These circumstances played an important role in the formation of the state of Urartu in the 9th century BCE. Many recent studies have pointed to the direct connection between the East-Caucasian peoples and Urartu and its people, known as Khalds. The place name "Dagaban", known from cuneiform inscriptions of the eighth century BCE, resembles the name Derbend. The multi-ethnic character of Urartu's population has also been mentioned, as well as the fact that the languages of these tribes or ethnic groups were related to those of the Caucasus and the Near East. For the time being this remains a hypothesis. Nevertheless, Daghestan and its peoples were directly or indirectly involved with the history of the state of Urartu. The state of Media (7th–6th centuries BCE) also played an important role in the destinies of the peoples of Daghestan (historical Caucasian Albania).

In the history of the Caucasus, and especially of Daghestan, one can also see the footsteps of the Cimmerians (end of 2nd–beginning of the 1st millennium BCE). But the traces of the Scythians (7th century BCE) in the historical and cultural development of the peoples of Daghestan are far more visible. They pushed out the Cimmerians and came to dominate the Northern Caucasus. At the same time they carried out raids into the Trans-Caucasian area and Near East. It is thought that after one such campaign some of the Scythians settled in the steppe areas of the Kura-Arax valley, and formed a state there which existed for a century. In this context it is very noticeable that the name of the river – "Dama" – in the language of the Tsakhurs (Yikiy-Albanians) is connected to the language of the Scythians. Its original name has survived in other languages genetically related to Tsakhur, for example, in Rutul: Nec', nec'ur; in Lezgin: Wac'.

Clearly, "Dama" (cf. "Don") is Scytho-Iranian in origin. Scythian culture in Daghestan is very well exhibited in archaeological excavations. And the Scythians themselves also borrowed some words from Daghestani languages, first of all in the spheres of phonetics and lexicon. Thus, for example, "pot" in the Ossetian language is clearly connected with the Rutul *haying*.

The ethno-cultural, socio-political, and economic development of the peoples of Daghestan (Caucasian Albania) during the first millennium BCE facilitated state unification. Evidently the formation of Caucasian Albania as a confederate state was a lengthy process. It was connected with the unique structure of the Daghestani village community, its development, the forms of ownership, and civil rights. The Daghestani village community was based on the equality of all its members, on collective communal ownership of summer and winter pastures, of forests, of rivers, and the fields further away from the village. The community (at its base very democratic) was governed by the *'adat*, the established tradition. The community had no slaves, only house servants.

Towards the second half of the 1st century BCE the Daghestani ethnoses and rural communities were both economically and politically ready to form a state in their own interests. In this respect the states of Urartu and Media were important examples. Judging by what we know of events, the formation of Caucasian Albania seems to have started already in the 5th century BCE. However, as a confederate state of 26 free, equal tribes Caucasian Albania finally evolved only towards the end of the third or the beginning of the second century BCE and existed until the tenth century CE. For about a millennium Caucasian Albania developed on a par with Armenia and Georgia in all spheres. The economic basis of Caucasian Albania was clearly better and more varied than the economies of Georgia and Armenia, while territorially it was larger than its neighbours. The south-eastern border of Caucasian Albania followed the Caspian Sea and the lower Kura and Arax rivers and its northern border was on the Terek. [4]

The formation of Caucasian Albania enabled the Daghestani peoples to cooperate with the countries of the Near and Middle East in economic, spiritual and also military spheres. With regard to the spiritual sphere, we note the acceptance by several Daghestani peoples, in the main speakers of languages of the Samur group (Yikiy-Albanians), of Zoroastrianism – the religion of the ancient tribes of Azerbaijan, Iran, and Central Asia. Zoroastrianism left a deep imprint on the way of life and material culture of the Tsakhurs, Rutuls, Kryzs, Budykhs, Kiurins and others. Many religious terms in the Tsakhur language are connected even now with Zoroastrianism. For example, *udžagli*, "religious leader", originally meant the keeper of the holy fire, the keeper of the temple of the holy fire. In the Tsakhur *auls* still today one can meet pantheons of ritual objects: the disc of the Sun with spreading rays, of the moon, of twinkling stars, of fire, etc. Such a pantheon was observed in the 1970s at the house of Ujah Muhammad in the village of Mukhakh. In olden times a niche was left in the houses to put the holy fire in. Zoroastrianism among the Daghestani peoples is an important feature in its own right and it is to be hoped that it will be fully studied some day.

The problem of the political structure of a confederate state of Caucasian Albania remains open as well. Strabo (1st century BCE) reports that in Albania "one king rules over all. Previously each people with its own language had its own king". This account obviously stands in need of correction. When Strabo calls the ruler of Caucasian Albania "king" we must give this term a tentative meaning. The ethnoses speaking their own languages had their elected plenipotentiaries representing free democratic communities. The head of the confederate state was probably elected either from amongst them or from a particular clan. These traditions survived in the election of the Tsakhur rulers and the Sultans of Il-lisu (15th–19th centuries).

Caucasian Albania was replaced in the tenth century by feudal principalities. This process should be regarded as the regular continuation of the established institutions of Caucasian Albania in changed circumstances: the advent of Islam and the encouragement by the conquerors of the formation of feudal ethnic units. The earliest epigraphic evidence from the period of islamization of Daghestan already testifies to this. In this respect the following inscription from the village of Mishlesh is a good example:

(1) The places of worship of Allah, and therefore do not acknowledge anyone together with Allah! The building of this

(2) blessed mosque was ordered by the great Amir Badal b. Mallah, may Allah accept his prayer

(3) and that of his parents! Written down on the date of the blessed month of Allah Dhu al-Hijja 644 [April-May 1247].

(4) The master Hasan b. Muhammad [...]. This inscription was written by ʿAli b. Malik.

(5) She is the wife of Amir Badal, Badin [?]-Khatun the daughter of Dhalla.[5]

The ancient contacts of Daghestan (the Caucasus) with the Near and Middle East also influenced greatly the written traditions of the peoples of Daghestan. The Albanian alphabet is generally believed to have been created in 430 CE. There are several documents known written in the Albanian alphabet, in particular a text found in 1937 by I. Abuladze in Echmiadzin and fragments of a document discovered in archaeological excavations in Mingechauri. (It should be noted that these were the historical lands of the Yikiy-Albanians and that the left bank of the Kura was until 1947 their traditional winter pasture.) Documents in the Albanian alphabet have also been found in the monastery of Leki, in Upper Labko and in other places. The Albanian alphabet was however created not in 430 but long before. What happened in 430 was a reform of a consonant-based alphabet into one with vowels as well, and its direction of writing was changed – instead of being written from right to left it was now to be written from left to right.

The Daghestani peoples had until 430 had their own alphabet based on the Aramaic system of writing. A fragment of a document written in this alphabet (a relic of a stone amulet) was discovered by the present author in the village of Ikhrek (the most ancient Rutul village) in July 1974. The amulet is a rectangular polished black agate (6 x 4 cm) adjusted for wearing on the chest. On its front side it has two circles in clear lines. Three horizontal and three vertical lines divide the right-hand circle into sixteen cells. Each cell apart from four incomplete cells on the sides contains one letter. The twelve letters along the vertical and horizontal lines obviously make up some words, which are connected with the purpose of the amulet. A preliminary study does not make it possible to connect these signs to any known alphabet. At the same time several signs have some resemblance to the letters of the Albanian alphabet. The left-hand circle is divided only by three horizontal lines. Here there are also twelve letters, significantly different from the signs of the right-hand circle. Unfortunately the signs inside the left-hand circle are damaged and their decipherment is very difficult. The amulet seems to be connected to the pre-Islamic religions of the area, in particular to Christianity, and is a valuable echo of the early system of writing in use among the peoples of Daghestan.[6] Together with their own alphabet the peoples of Daghestan, especially merchants and traders, made wide use also of the Persian and Aramaic alphabets (second half of the 1st millennium BCE–3rd century CE).

The creation of the confederate state of Caucasian Albania was also connected with the official conversion of the peoples of Daghestan to Christianity (313 CE). According to many scholars one of the Daghestani peoples – the Tsakhurs – lived in the past on the larger part of the territory of Caucasian Albania. In the South East they occupied historically Artsakh (Aran-Tsakh). In the South West the border has remained basically the same until today, although with certain changes in favour of Georgia (the Shirakh steppes along the lower Yori river, called by the Tsakhurs Gabri, from K'abri). The territory of the Tsakhurs within Caucasian Albania was the metropolis in relation to other regions.

The self-designation of the Tsakhurs is *yikiy*. The analysis of the ethnic names of the peoples of the Eastern Caucasus, as well as the plural morphemes in the terms of relationship in several Daghestani languages, shows clearly that the ethnonym *yigbi* and its phonetic variation *ahqbi, ahaqar* are structurally changed variants of a single ancient ethnonym for the peoples of the Eastern Caucasus. Especially striking is the semantic and material community in the morphological and phonetic structure of the present ethnonyms of the peoples of the Eastern Caucasus. For example, the ethnonyms *yi-q'-bi* – Tsakhurs; *aq'a-hg'-bi, ag'a-hg'ar* – Rutuls; *u-han-ur* – Tabasarans; *bu-duh-ar* – Buduhs; *qir-ic'-ar* – Kryzs; *a-gul-ar* – Aguls; *ya-hul-ar* – Laks; *c'a-h'ar-aguš* – Dargins; *vai-nah* – Chechens (literally "our people"); *nah-chuo* – Chechens; *nuh-chi* – fellow-tribesmen. The root sounds *q, x, q', ğ* have a material community and probably originate in the Eastern Caucasian **q'l/ *q'w*. The determined shaping of the initial basis by the elements *n, l, r, d* in the various languages is justified by the structural peculiarities of the East Caucasian languages. This idea is confirmed in the plural morphemes, as we see in the terms of familiarity, for example: *q'ar, qar* in Tabasaran, *q'al, qal* in Dargin, *qun, xun* in Rutul, *q'a* in Tsakhur.

The full initial meaning of the ethnonyms of the East Caucasian people has survived in the personal pronouns in the Borchin-Khin dialect. For example: "we" – *yanur* (inclusive), *yugnar < yi-gun-ar* (exclusive); "you" – *wi* (exclusive) – in this particular example there is an anomaly: the pronoun *wi < *wi-n-ar* "we" in the Borchin-Khinov dialect should be seen as the inclusive; "you" – *wugnar < *wu-gun-ar* (inclusive). And so the ethnic names of the peoples of the Eastern Caucasus mean "we", "we – people", "we – the people".[7]

The continuous close contacts with the Near and Middle East, and with the peoples of Semitic speech, indeed accommodated the early spread of Christianity in the Caucasus. Officially Christianity was adopted by Armenia in 302, by Caucasian Albania in 313, by Georgia in 317 CE. The conditions for the early spread of Christianity in Armenia, Georgia and Caucasian Albania were absolutely identical. The early spread of Christianity in the Caucasus is connected, in particular, with the existence of a Jewish diaspora there. The first settlers arrived as early as the 6th-5th centuries BCE during the Babylonian exile. After 539 BCE, when the Persian king Cyrus took Babylon and allowed Jews to return to their homeland, some of them remained with Cyrus and in due time changed over to the use of Persian. When sizeable population groups from Persia were moved to the Caucasus, Jews probably formed an important part of them. The Persian colonisers settled in the main in the piedmont opposite the passes across the main Caucasian range: in Majalis, Derbend, Mamrash, Quba, Shamakhi, Kakhi, Sheki, Jinykh. Also the riddle of the Ten Lost Tribes may be explained by the constant movement to the Caucasus of settlers from the Near and Middle East. The Jews in this region maintained the Law of Moses in all its purity and honoured it as sacred. The most influential and educated among them lived in expectation of the Messiah – the anointed saviour and king.

The belief in the Messiah was an important dogma of Old Testament Judaism. Messianic expectations were especially strong in the first century BCE. They reinforced migration processes and augmented the stream of Jews into Caucasian Albania (Daghestan). This was also facilitated by Roman expansion.[8] Traditions have survived of Jewish participation in the struggle of the Yikiy-Albanians against the Romans during the campaigns of Lucullus (74–66 BCE) and Pompey (66 BCE) in the Caucasus. The correspondence between Pompey and the king of the Albanians was apparently conducted with the active participation of Jews, who knew the Yikiy-Albanian (Gargarian) language as well as Aramaic (Syriac), Persian and, most probably, Latin. Even today memories of the ancient past link many settlements in Daghestan and Azerbaijan to Jewish origins. The names most respected among the Daghestani peoples are Ibrahim (Abraham), Musa (Moses), Davud (David), Maryam (Miriam) etc. Many illustrious families in the Caucasus claim descent from the house of David; one of them is the famous family of Bagrationi, who supplied both Armenia and Georgia with kings.

Pre-Islamic Daghestan (Caucasian Albania) developed along the same path as the rest of the Near and Middle East. The Caucasus became in the main Christian. Armenia, Georgia, and Caucasian Albania received not only the reformed alphabet through St. Mesrop Mashtots, but also the New Testament in their native languages. Spiritual, mainly hagiographic, historical and juridical literature developed in the local languages; religious structures (monasteries, churches and schools) were built; and missionary work was pursued actively. The 5th–8th centuries were especially fertile. Between the 4th and 7th centuries CE the Huns, who settled along the Caspian lowlands, adopted Christianity as a result of the missionary activity of the Albanian Church and the Bible was translated into the Hun language.

The intensified christianisation of the peoples of the Caucasus was halted and then reversed by the arrival of the new world religion, Islam. Arab expansion into the Caucasus started in the 640s but the region of Caucasian Albania closest to the Caspian was islamised only by the eleventh century. The first Islamic *madrasa* (school) in the Caucasus was opened in 1075 by the Seljuk *wazir* Nizam al-Mulk in Tsakhur. In order to spread Islam, books on Muslim jurisprudence were translated into the Tsakhur language. Nevertheles, the islamization of the peoples of Daghestan took several centuries. Nowadays among the Caucasian peoples Christianity has deep roots among the Armenians (the Gregorian church) and the Georgians (the Orthodox church). Among the peoples of the Daghestani group of languages the Udins are followers of Christianity.

A special place in the pre-Islamic history of Daghestan and the interaction of its peoples with those of the Near and Middle East was occupied by the ancient city of Derbend. Nowadays it is by territory and population the second largest city in the Republic of Daghestan. It is 5,000 years old. It was established on the western shore of the Caspian where the mountains of the main Caucasian range reach almost to the sea leaving only a narrow path, "the gate". According to the sources the name Derbend dates back to the 6th century CE and is connected to the Persian word meaning "lock, door-lock".[9] Apart from the name "Derbend" the city had more than a dozen other names, including Chor, Chol, Churul, Chulli, Tsur, Bab al-Abwab, Bab al-Hadid, Kakhulga, Demyr-Gapy (or Temir-Kapy). Derbend was constructed as a large and important fortress mainly in the 6th century CE. Even today its architecture arouses the admiration of the viewer by its size and strength. Derbend is the great textbook of the history of Daghestan: Rome, the Parthians, Iran, the Byzantines, the Arab Caliphate, the Khazar Kaganate, the Seljuks, Timur, the Golden Horde, the Safavids, the Ottomans, and many others wished to control it. By virtue of its historical significance, its cultural heritage, its economic and other parameters, and especially its ethnic composition, Derbend is the most important centre in Daghestan.

One final question connected to the islamization of Daghestan has to be dealt with: why did Caucasian Albania fail in what Armenia and Georgia were able to do, to retain its Christianity, that is to remain Christian countries neighbouring on and even surrounded by the Islamic world?

The islamization of Daghestan began after the disintegration of the confederate state of the Daghestani peoples (i.e., after the tenth century). The primary reason for the loss of Christianity by the Daghestani peoples was the lack of a strong centralised government. The very political structure of Caucasian Albania contained seeds of disunity. In addition to the ethno-linguistic regions certain other regions had developed – like Chog, Uti, Artsakh, Lipina, Maskut, Paytakaran – which could at any time form an opposition to the central (confederate) government. And that is what happened in fact: the confederation could not withstand the strong blows inflicted by the Arabs, and still more by the Seljuk Turks. Historical Caucasian Albania disintegrated and was replaced by a string of feudal principalities. These circumstances led to the enfeeblement of the Albanian church. And yet the Albanian church existed and even played a significant part in the affairs of the peoples of Daghestan – including the islamized ones – until the first half of the nineteenth century.

NOTES

1   G. Kh. Ibragimov, *Rutul'skii iazyk* (Moscow, 1978), pp. 7-9.
2   R. M. Magomedov, *Istoriia Dagestana* (Makhachkala, 1968), pp. 16-7; *Lingvisticheskii entsiklopedicheskii slovar* (Moscow, 1990), pp. 538, 570, 572.
3   Magomedov, *op. cit.*, pp. 7-14.
4   There are also other points of view about the borders of Caucasian Albania; see F. Mamedova, *Politicheskaia i istoricheskaia geografiia Kavkazskoi Albanii* (Baku, 1986), p. 8.
5   L. I. Lavrov, *Epigraficheskie pamiatniki Severnogo Kavkaza*, Pt. *1, X – XVII vv.* (Moscow, 1966), p. 82, 276.
6   Ibragimov, *op. cit.*, pp. 189-90.
7   Ibid., pp. 258-65; id., 'K voprosu obshchnosti nazvanii Vostochno-Kavkazskikh narodov', in *Tipologiia i teoriia iazyka* (Moscow, 1995).
8   Garun Ibragimov, 'Khristianstvo i tsakhury', *Al'fa i Omega*, (Moscow), 1999, No. 1.
9   Cf. the (originally Persian) word *darwaza* in the languages of Southern Daghestan meaning "gate".

ABU MUSLIM IN ISLAMIC HISTORY AND MYTHOLOGY OF THE NORTHERN CAUCASUS[1]

VLADIMIR BOBROVNIKOV

In this paper I aim to offer a re-evaluation of the role of Abu Muslim in the dissemination of Islam among the Caucasian highlanders. This has of course nothing to do with 'Abd al-Rahman ibn Muslim, the famous 'Abbasid general, a real political and religious leader from early medieval Khorasan, better known as Abu Muslim, who never came to the Caucasus before his murder in 755. My study deals with a more legendary local Muslim hero. Virtually all Daghestani and many Chechen Muslims believe him to have introduced the Islamic faith and Islamic rule among their ancestors. I shall argue that his image is very relevant to a deeper understanding of a twofold historical and mythological dimension of islamization in the northern Caucasus. The investigation of historical narratives and religious practices related to Abu Muslim inevitably leads us to a number of important problems, such as the principal periods and actors of islamization in this region, the cultural and political links between the pre-modern northern Caucasus, Central Asia, the Middle East and Iran, the Shi'i influence on late medieval Daghestan, and the Islamic transformation of pre-Muslim holy places.

From the methodological point of view, I propose in this article a new diachronic comparative approach to the whole complex of sources relating to Abu Muslim in the northern Caucasus. To date, only medieval Arabic chronicles have been used for the study of the islamization of Daghestan. The bulk of modern ethnographic data about holy places associated with Abu Muslim in Highland Daghestan remains under-researched. In order to make a start at filling this serious lacuna, I have used both written sources and oral histories collected in the northern Caucasus from the late 19th to the beginning of the 21st century. My sources include Arabic manuscripts and inscriptions relating to Abu Muslim and other heroes of the process of islamization, descriptions of rites practised in the holy places associated with Abu Muslim, and their microtoponymy in Avar and other Daghestani languages. This article is based mainly on first-hand materials obtained during my fieldwork in Daghestan in the period 1992–1997.

A HISTORICO-CRITICAL APPROACH TO ABU MUSLIM IN DAGHESTAN

The historiographical treatment of Abu Muslim has changed considerably over the last two centuries. Initially he was regarded as the first Arab conqueror and Muslim missionary in the Caucasus. Such a view can be found in Muslim chronicles (Ar. *tawarikh*) of Daghestan like the famous *Derbend-nameh*, *Ta'rikh Daghistan* or *Ta'rikh Abi Muslim*, which were composed gradually over the period from the 10th to the early 20th centuries.[2] Below I outline the main elements of this narrative, focussing on those which are significant for the purposes of my study.

The *shaykh* 'Abd al-Rahman ibn 'Abd al-Malik Abu Muslim (or Abu al-Muslim) is said to have been an Arab nobleman and a descendant of the Prophet Muhammad (Ar. *sayyid*) through his uncles Hamza and 'Abbas. He was born in the Syrian town of Damascus and thus was referred to as *al-Dimashqi al-Shami*. Abu Muslim built a Friday mosque in Damascus and was the first to preach in it. When he was four years old, his father fell in battle as a martyr (Ar. *shahid*) "fighting for [the Shi'i *imam*] Husayn ibn 'Ali" against the Umayyad Caliph Marwan II. As soon as Abu Muslim grew up, he gathered an army "of five thousand men", avenged his father and left Syria for Shirvan and Daghestan. In a seven-year holy war (Ar. *jihad* and *ghazawat*) he conquered the North Caucasus including the remote lands of the Circassians. Abu Muslim converted the highlanders to Islam and built their first mosques. Leaving the Caucasus or dying of a wound (according to different versions of the story), he established Arab governors in all the major Daghestani settlements like the town of Derbend, and the villages of Qurush, Tsakhur, Richa, Qala-Quraysh, Ghazi-Ghumuq, Kubachi, Qhunzaqh. The ruling dynasties of the *shamkhal*s of Ghazi-Ghumuq, the *utsmi*s of Qaytaq (Qala-Quraysh), *ma'sum*s and *qadi*s of Tabasaran — that is to say, almost all the late medieval royal houses of Daghestan with the exception of the Avar *khan*s — claimed to be descendants of these governors and Abu Muslim's closest relatives.

With slight modifications this same story can be found in late pre-modern Arabic building inscriptions and even in contemporary oral histories from the North Caucasus. For instance, inhabitants of the Lezgin village of Akhty claim that their settlement was named after the sister (from the Arabic word *ukht*, meaning 'sister') of Abu Muslim, Umm al-Mu'minat, who is said to be buried near their Friday mosque.[3] On its southern wall is the following inscription, copied from an older one after the repair of the mosque in 1899:

> The commune (*jamaʿa*) of Akhty of the Samur district [of the Daghestan province — V.B.] re-built this Friday mosque on the very place of the older mosque which was built by the brave ruler (*malik*) ʿAbd al-Rahman al-Makki known as Abu Muslim al-Dimashqi al-Shami who conquered Daghestan...[4]

The inscription on the wall of the Friday mosque in the Daghestani village Richa reports:

> Abu Muslim left Damascus for Daghestan in the year 115 AH [733–4 CE], fought with them [infidel Daghestanis — V.B.] for the religion and built a number of mosques including this Friday mosque in Richa...[5]

In 1997 in the southern Daghestani village of Rutul I heard a similar story told by Navruz Khalifatov from a clan (Ir. *tuqhum*) claiming to be the descendants of Abu Muslim.

The earliest criticism of this narrative appeared in Daghestani and Russian historiography on the eve of the Russian conquest of the Caucasus. The 19th-century Azeri Muslim historian ʿAbbas-Quli-Agha Bakikhanov questioned the authenticity of the legend of Abu Muslim in his book *Gulistan-i Iram*. So did his younger Daghestani colleague Hasan Efendi al-Alqadari in his historical treatise *Athar-i Daghistan*, where he pointed out serious errors in the narrative about Abu Muslim.[6] The Russian historian N.V. Khanykov established that the authors of medieval Daghestani chronicles often confused Abu Muslim with Maslama, the son of the Umayyad caliph ʿAbd al-Malik (r. 685–705 CE) and the brother of the caliphs al-Walid I (r. 705–715 CE) and Hisham (r. 724-743 CE). Even his name is made up out of the first name of the Khorasani hero and the name of the father of Maslama. In fact, almost all the campaigns ascribed to Abu Muslim were organized by Maslama starting from the end of the 7th century, at a time when the real Abu Muslim had not yet been born.[7] Similar errors in the story about Abu Muslim were pointed out by Mirza Kazem-beg, the eminent 19th-century historian of Caucasian origin.

In the 20th century the story about Abu Muslim's activities in the Caucasus was scrupulously examined by V. Minorsky, M.-S. Saidov, A. Shikhsaidov, T. Aitberov, A. Krishtopa, A. Alikberov and other scholars of the period. Their studies revealed that the famous Abu Muslim from Khorasan had almost nothing in common with the Daghestani *shaykh* known by the same name. The arguments of advocates of a historico-critical approach to the story about Abu Muslim are the following: first, the hero from Khorasan was of humble Iranian origin and could not have belonged to the noble tribe of Quraysh. Secondly, Abu Muslim is reported to have organized military campaigns which lasted for hundreds of years from 709 (i.e., a long time before his birth) to 912 or even 1256 (respectively 157 or 501 years after his death). Thirdly, holy places (Ir. *pir*/Ar. *ziyarat*) related to the *shaykh* emerged either before the very advent of Islam or in the late Middle Ages. Last but not least, in reality, the *shamkhal*s, the *utsmi*s and other royal houses claiming to be descendants of Abu Muslim's relatives and companions date back only to a period following the Mongol conquest of the Caucasus. Their local titles begin to appear in the epigraphic materials of the 13th–15th centuries.[8]

From such a perspective, the story about Abu Muslim in the Caucasus seems to have something of the character of fairy tales. Most contemporary historians and anthropologists believe him to be a pure fiction of late Muslim literature. Today there is a strong consensus that there was no such religious and political leader in the past of the Caucasus.

In my opinion, such a hypercritical view of the rigid dualism of fiction and reality is not much better than the approach of late Muslim historiography. It is damaged by a dangerous misuse of pre-modern Muslim sources from the North Caucasus. It does not take into account the crucial differences between modern European and medieval Muslim approaches to historical writing as such. This should be pointed out especially with reference to the so-called Muslim "chronicles" originating from pre-modern Daghestan. In fact this genre is not historical literature *pur et dur*, but a kind of political (and sometimes also legal) pamphlet.[9] As a rule, the authors of these works used historical data for contemporary political purposes. They wanted to legitimize the rights of local Muslim noblemen (Turk. *khan*s, *bek*s) or village communes (Ar. *jama'at*) to power and territories. For this reason it seems not to be very fruitful to analyse these sources merely with the aim of discovering 'what really happened'.

ACTORS OF ISLAMIZATION IN THE CULTURAL MEMORY OF THE MUSLIM COMMUNITY

I propose instead to focus on the image of actors of islamization as these are reflected in the local Muslim 'cultural memory'. This term as such was first proposed by the French sociologist Maurice Halbwachs, who developed the concept of '*mémoire collective*' in the 1920s, and then reconsidered in a post-modernist sense by Jan Assmann, specializing in Egyptian studies, in our own time. Assmann has pointed out that the common 'cultural memory [*das kulturelle Gedächtnis*] of a shared inhabited past' is essential for the identity of a community. Independent of its historical validity, such a memory is always a social construct whose features result from the need to make sense of particular realities and from their referential framework.[10] In this context, the significance of narratives is measured less by their historical validity than by their function within the cultural memory. 'One only has to realize', as Assmann states, 'that memory has nothing to do with historical sciences'.[11]

From chronicles and oral histories it may be deduced that Abu Muslim is a kind of 'collective actor' of islamization in the northern Caucasus. We can guess that his attributes were derived from different Muslim missionaries of both foreign and local origin. It is significant that we can list a dozen (!) holy places and tombs associated either with the *shaykh* himself or with his close relatives in Highland Daghestan alone. According to the *Ta'rikh Daghistan* by Muhammad Mulla-Rafi', there were five Arab *shaykh*s originating from the tribe of the Prophet who came to Daghestan from Syria and converted the Caucasian highlanders to Islam. This chronicle mentions two different *shaykh*s referred to as Abu Muslim (or 'Abd al-Muslim). The first of them ruled over the Avar village of Qhunzaqh following the death of the last descendant of the five Arab *shaykh*s. Another Abu al-Muslim was also an Avar ruler and the grandson of the first one.[12] Similar stories are reproduced in numerous Avar village chronicles like the anonymous *Ta'rikh Maza*. Occasionally, the Arab origin of Abu Muslim is not mentioned. He is reported to have been an heir of Arab missionaries who perished as *shahid*s during holy wars against local 'infidels' headed by the Avar ruler (Av. *nutsall nusal*) Suraqa:

> ... imam being the holder of a naked sword and greatly distinguished shaykh Ahmad, (shaykh) 'Abdallah and (shaykh) 'Abd al-Muslim converted to Islam Ghara-Khaytaq [the highland state of Qara-Qaytaq — V.B.]..., they diffused Islam from Ghara-Khaytaq to Chir-Yurt, where ruled Qakhar, the brother of Suraqa. And they killed him [Qakhar — V.B.] and destroyed his habitation and burnt his fortress. Then they returned home from this campaign. Then shaykh Ahmad and 'Abdallah were killed and only 'Abd al-Muslim was still alive. Then 'Abd al-Muslim accompanied by his army moved against Suraqa, who had stayed in the Highlands. Soon afterward 'Abd al-Muslim killed him, seized all his treasures, burnt his fortresses and installed himself in Avaria as the imam of all Daghestan and all the Muslims... This dates back to the year 654 [1256].[13]

Historical notes like those quoted above reveal a complicated character of this genre. Both real and mythological materials relating to different historical periods are thoroughly mixed together in them. In the same passage we find real Arab generals like Maslama and late Daghestani missionaries and mythological personages like the Avar *nutsal* Suraqa. Although known under the pure Muslim name of Suraqa, he is criticized in Muslim Daghestani historiography as a symbol of the 'criminal, sinful and infidel ruler'.[14] On the other hand, the historical validity of a story about the *shaykh* Abu Muslim of Qhunzaqh is affirmed by the eleventh-century Sufi treatise *Rayhan al-Haqa'iq wa-Bustan al-Daqa'iq* composed by Abu Bakr Muhammad al-Darbandi. We might agree with the contemporary Moscow historian A.K. Alikberov, who assumes that the image of Abu Muslim as it is reflected in the cultural memory of the Caucasian Muslims is based mostly on the attributes of a local Shafi'i preacher (Ar. *khatib*) and ascetic missionary (Ar. *zahid*) called by the same name, who spread Islam in the north-eastern Caucasus in the 10th–early 11th centuries and is mentioned in the book of al-Darbandi.[15] Dying in a war for the sake of Islam, this *shaykh* may have been buried in Qhunzaqh, where his *ziyara*, situated in a domed mausoleum near the Friday mosque, soon became a place of pilgrimage and is much venerated even now. Shortly after his death there appeared a lot of tales about miracles performed at the Qhunzaqh mausoleum. From the eleventh century the name of Abu Muslim was included in 'the ranks of (local Muslim) saints' (Ar. *tabaqat al-awliya*').

While examining the image of Abu Muslim, we should keep in mind that his attributes relate to different stages of the islamization of the Caucasus. I distinguish here three main periods[16] in this historical process of the "*longue durée*" over more than a thousand years. The first one ran parallel with the Arab conquests from the late seventh to the tenth centuries. It was associated with a long-lasting struggle between the Arab caliphate and the Khazar khaqanate reflected in local Muslim chronicles.[17] Its main actors were Arab generals and kings including Salman ibn Rabi'a (d. in the mid-7th century), Maslama ibn 'Abd al-Malik and their successors like Abu 'Ubayda Jarrah ibn 'Abdallah al-Hakami, killed by the Khazars during his campaign of 730, and the Umayyad Caliphs Hisham ibn 'Abd al-Malik and Marwan b. Muhammad b. Marwan, who ruled over Transcaucasia and organized at least six campaigns to Daghestan in 732–39. In the cultural memory of the Caucasian Muslims their actions were attributed to Abu Muslim.[18] The Arab expansion resulted in the military victory of Islam on the territory of contemporary Azerbaijan and southern Daghestan.

The second stage of the islamization started in the tenth century and took about six hundred years. In this period the Caucasus witnessed a number of great new conquests, including the advent of the Turkic Seljuq tribes in the tenth-eleventh centuries, the Mongol invasions in the mid-twelfth century and campaigns by the *amir* Timur (r. 1370–1405). Although the Mongol invasion seriously hampered the diffusion of Islam, islamization was soon encouraged by Mongol *khan*s who were newly converted to Islam. By the sixteenth century the whole of Daghestan had become a predominantly Muslim area (Ar. *dar al-islam*). Separate Muslim rulers and communes appeared in Chechnya, Ingushetia and among the Circassian tribes. The Daghestani chronicles recalled all these conquerors under the generic name of 'the Turks'.[19] The *Ta'rikh Abi Muslim* includes a report about the *Shirvan-shah* Isma'il al-Darbandi (r. 1382–1417) who took part in the holy wars organised by Timur, but it turns him into the son of Abu Muslim.

From the tenth century onwards the main actors of islamization were local missionaries who carried Islam to areas which had never been under Arab rule. These missionaries included rulers, scholars, merchant travellers and even shepherds. The cultural memory of the Caucasian Muslims turned them all into relatives and companions (Ar. *ashab*) of Abu Muslim. Between the tenth and the sixteenth centuries a narrative concerning numerous fictitious sons of Abu Muslim and detailed genealogies of their 'noble descendants' (Ar. *nasab*) was incorporated into the Daghestani chronicles.[20] At the same time, there appeared oral histories reporting how Abu Muslim dispatched his relatives and Arab companions to propagate Islam among the Daghestani and Chechen highlanders.[21] Apart from the *shaykh*'s sister referred to above, there are holy tombs of two cousins of Abu Muslim both called Musa and venerated in the Andi village of Ashali and the Qumyq village of Endirey in northern Daghestan. According to local legend, Abu Muslim sent both *shaykh*s to convert the Andis to Islam, but Musa of Ashali was killed by a man from the Gukuchilal clan, and his cousin had to flee from the village of Andi to Endirey in the Lowlands. The tomb of another *shaykh*, Muhammad, who is said to have been the younger brother of Abu Muslim, is venerated in the Avar village of Miatly in northern Daghestan.[22] In almost every Daghestani village and in some Chechen villages one can still hear numerous oral narratives about clans of descendants of the *shaykh* and Friday mosques built by him.

From the very beginning local Sufis played an important role in the islamization of the region.[23] According to what Muhammad al-Darbandi and early Arab geographers tell us, *shay-*

*kh*s of different Sufi brotherhoods (Ar. *tariqat*) were installed in the Caucasus at least in the tenth and the eleventh centuries. The writings of Sufi leaders, particularly those of al-Ghazali (d. 505/1111) were studied and copied in Muslim schools and academies (Ar. *madrasa*s) throughout Azerbaijan and southern Daghestan. Sufi lodges (Ar.-Pers. *khanaqah*s), which are known in the area from the eleventh century onwards, became the centres of Islamic knowledge (Ar. *al-marakiz al-islamiyya*). Their rapid diffusion in the Highlands is attested by a famous Arabic building inscription from the village of Rutul, which reports that

> ... 'Abd al-Samad, the son of Nalki [?], ordered the building of this khanaqah in the month of Muharram of the year 545 [May1150].[24]

In the eleventh–thirteenth centuries *khanaqah*s also served as missionary centres and as a kind of fortress (Ar. *ribat*) which formed a 'highland wall' (Turk. *dagh-barı*) 40 kilometres in length to the north of Derbend inhabited by militant Sufis fighting in the holy war (Ar. *ghuzat*).[25] Ruins of many such *ribat*s can still be seen in southern Daghestan.

In the light of these realities, it is easy to detect a distinct Sufi influence on narratives and religious practices associated with Abu Muslim. In a number of village chronicles Abu Muslim is confused with Amir Qalandar, 'the son of Sultan Haydar and descendant of Hamza al-'Arabi'. The late medieval gravestone attributed to Amir Qalandar was situated in the Lak village of Ghazi-Ghumuq until it disappeared in the mid-twentieth century. Despite the difference in names, both Abu Muslim and Amir Qalandar are reported to have had the same *sayyid* genealogy, the same wanderings before their arrival in Daghestan, and to have engaged in the same missionary activities in the Caucasus.[26] Apparently the name Amir Qalandar was derived from the Iranian word *qalandar*, which means 'wandering Sufi' or 'travelling ascetic'. The term was widespread in the Muslim world at least from the eleventh century. The *Akhty-nameh* also reports a marriage between the sister of Abu Muslim and the Iranian ruler Darwishaya, his name being derived from the Iranian term *darwish*, with a meaning identical to that of *qalandar*. Moreover, Daghestani holy places often contain wooden sticks attributed to Abu Muslim, or his relatives or companions. One such rod with a metallic end is kept in a long wooden box in the mausoleum of *shaykh* Abu Muslim in Qhunzaqh. I have also observed a similar stick wrapped in red cloth and placed in a *ziyarat* venerated in the village of Rutul. It is associated with the Sufi Havali, the woman saint who is said to have been the wife of an Arab companion of Abu Muslim and the founder of the local clan of Sefier (Rut. 'the Sufis').[27] As is well known, a rod or stick is always associated with a Sufi. It is interesting that the Arabic term for 'rod' (*'asa*) has been borrowed into almost all the Daghestani languages.[28] Another material attribute of Sufi *shaykhs* can be found in the mausoleum in Qhunzaqh. This is a typical Sufi dress (Ar. *khirqa*) dating back to the sixteenth century.

Islamization was linked with both peaceful and militant activities of Muslim missionaries. According to local written tradition, it was often associated with holy wars between village communes and khanates competing for power and lands. Muslim communities which had recently converted to Islam conducted regular warfare with their 'infidel' neighbours over their lands, referring to them as the 'territory of war' (Ar. *dar al-harb*). An amazing description of such a war can be found in the *Ta'rikh Daghistan* by Muhammad Mulla-Rafi':

> Thus the Muslims subjugated all the areas of highlanders or Daghestan partly by enslavement, revenge, assassination and destruction; partly by peace [Ar. Islam — V.B.], settlement [of Muslims — V.B.] and concessions... a war begun between them [infidels — V.B.] and Muslims. Hostility and conflicts continued for fourteen years. At last they [the infidels — V.B.] exhausted all their stocks, their life became hard, they did not want to fight any more, the warfare horrified them. Then they became faithful and converted to Islam.[29]

Even more spectacular is the cultural memory of the violence practised in the second stage of islamization as reflected in rituals associated with holy places of Abu Muslim. For example, a sword attributed to Abu Muslim was kept in the mosque of the Kalanib quarter of the Avar village of Chokh before the 1940s. Starting at Qurban-Bayram the inhabitants of Chokh used to go to the outskirts of their village facing the neighbouring village of Ruguja. There the *mu'adhdhin* (Turk./Dag. *budun*) broke a pot by the sword of Abu Muslim. At the same time he recited the profession of faith (Ar. *shahada*) three times and asked God to give abundant crops to the Muslims of Chokh and to destroy the prosperity of the Tushins (i.e. Christians) from Ruguja.[30]

Oral histories and religious practices connected to Abu Muslim are also reflected in the third stage of islamization. It lasted from the late sixteenth to the early nineteenth centuries. Following the conversion to Islam of the Daghestanis and then the Chechens, there occurred a gradual transformation of highland society and culture. From the sixteenth century, Daghestan, where the process of islamization had a relatively profound effect, became an important pan-Caucasian centre of Arab-Muslim knowledge and missionary activities. In the context of the struggle for the Caucasus between Sunni Muslim Ottoman Turkey, Shiʻi Iran and Christian Russia, Islam acquired an important political dimension. The resistance of the highlanders to the Russian and Iranian advances in the northern Caucasus was regarded as a permanent holy war against 'infidels' (Ar. *kuffar*), Shiʻi 'heretics' (Ar. *rawafid*) and local 'hypocrites' (Ar. *munafiqun*) who supported them.[31] The warrior (Ar. *ghazi*) became the main actor of this time. In the local cultural memory *ghazi*s of the nineteenth-century Caucasian war are often confused with companions (Ar. *ashab*) of Abu Muslim. From the sixteenth century onwards there appear a great many so-called 'saints' cemeteries' or '*ghazis*' cemeteries' throughout Daghestan and Chechnya. These are simple gravestones or more rarely small mausolea dating from the seventeenth to the mid-twentieth centuries. Local oral tradition often reports 'forty martyrs who perished in holy war', like those buried in the southern Daghestani village of Dibgalik or 'forty less one martyrs' (*shuhada*) buried near the Darghin village of Usisha.[32]

PRE-MODERN DAGHESTAN AND THE ARAB WORLD

Modern Caucasian studies, especially in Western Europe, have long been dominated by approaches based on the view that the Caucasian margins were isolated from the Islamic centres of the Muslim world. Such an assumption dates back to the Russian conquest of the northern Caucasus in the mid-nineteenth century, when there appeared real political and cultural barriers separating this region from the Ottoman Empire and the other Muslim areas of the Middle East. As a result, there is still a widespread, and completely erroneous, view of the pre-modern northern Caucasus as a 'backward' and 'primitive periphery' of the Muslim world.

Materials relating to the cult of Abu Muslim allow us to re-evaluate this misleading notion. Of course, it is no part of my intention here to argue for the genuineness of the fictitious Arab genealogies of the Daghestani royal houses. These are nothing but fiction (though based on a perverted reality). In reality, pre-modern Daghestan as the Islamic centre of the northern Caucasus was linked with the cultural and political centres of the Muslim Middle East. In the late 1930s the eminent Russian scholar A.N. Genko assumed that the links between the Arab diaspora in the eastern Caucasus and the Middle East dated back to the seventeenth century. Epigraphic, archaeological and ethnographic evidence discovered in Highland Daghestan by the end of the twentieth century has proved that these contacts developed at least from the tenth to the eighteenth centuries.[33]

One of the main channels of such contacts was the Arabs who lived in the northern Caucasus. The account given in the *Derbend-nameh* of 24,000 Arab warriors (*ghazi*s) from Syria settled by Maslama in four quarters of Derbend is confirmed both by local and Arab narrative sources and by toponymic and ethnographic data. It is likely that the number of settlers is exaggerated, but it was also certainly significant. A considerable community was established in Derbend and its environs at the time of the Arab military campaigns by the mid-eighth century. They inhabited many *ribat*s of the *Dagh-barı* line of fortification which defended the northern borders of the Arab-Muslim caliphate. According to the anonymous *Ta'rikh Shirvan wal-Bab*, Arab immigrants in the Caucasus undertook a number of raids (Ar. *ghazawat*) against 'highland infidels' of Daghestan in the third century AH (mid-ninth century).[34] The legacy of these settlers was felt in the local cultural memory up to the 1930s, when people from the Tat village of Dar-Wag, 35 km to the west of Derbend, still claimed Arabic as their native tongue.[35] Contacts between Daghestan and Syria dating from the first stage of islamization were recorded in a myth about the Syrian origin of Muslim dynasties of Daghestan. The legend claims that Abu Muslim appointed a nobleman from the village of Khal in Syria (Ar. *al-Sham*) as his regent; this then lay behind the Ghazi-Ghumuq ruler's title of Shamkhal.[36]

Another tale contained in the *Ta'rikh Daghistan* and the *Ta'rikh Maza* about the arrival of descendants of Hamza and 'Abbas in the northern Caucasus in the second or third centuries AH (8th–9th centuries CE) is not so fantastic as might appear. Arab immigrants continued to settle in the area during the second stage of islamization. Individual Arabs arrived in the Caucasus even in the eighteenth and the nineteenth centuries. If warriors prevailed among the first immigrants, most of the later settlers were well-educated Muslim scholars from Syria, Egypt and, especially, Yemen.[37] Azeri and Daghestani *madrasa*s played the role of international centres of scholarship. Some of them, like the Nizamiyya *madrasa* in Tsakhur in southern Daghestan, called after its founder the famous Nizam al-Mulk, the *wazir* of the Seljuq Sultan Alp-Arslan (r. 1063–72), were well known in the Muslim world.[38]

Arabic sources of the fifteenth century tell us of *madrasa*s in Derbend and in the Daghestani villages of Kubachi, Ghumuq and Qhunzaqh.[39] Many Arab immigrants claimed to be
descendants of the Prophet Muhammad (Ar. *sada, ashraf*), thus asserting an identity that allowed them to gain prestigious positions in the Caucasian Muslim communities. A relevant
example of such settlers is the *sayyid shaykh* Ahmad al-Yamani (originating from Yemen),
who had lectured at the famous university of al-Azhar in Egypt before he was sent by an
'Abbasid Caliph to preach Islam in Daghestan. He settled in the Lak village of Ghazi-Ghumuq where he became a *qadi* and teacher renowned for his proselytizing activities among
the highlanders. His descendants lived in Ghazi-Ghumuq till the early nineteenth century.
At the beginning of the twentieth century there still existed the Yemeni cemetery (Lak *Ya-
manittal*) in Ghazi-Ghumuq.[40] Similar Arab cemeteries are attested in many other Daghestani villages.

Another important channel of cultural exchange between the northern Caucasus and
the Middle East was that formed by Daghestanis who travelled in the Arab world both on
pilgrimages and for study at the leading centres of Muslim knowledge in the Hijaz, Syria, Egypt, Iraq and Yemen. Though interrupted in periods of great foreign invasions, these
links are attested at least from the eleventh or the twelfth century. Late medieval scholars called Daghestan a 'sea of sciences' (Ar. *bahr al-'ulum*). Manuscript collections, recently
discovered in Highland Daghestan by expeditions led by Professor A.R. Shikhsaidov, provide us with a long list of Caucasian '*ulama*' who graduated from al-Azhar and other Muslim universities of the Arab world and were 'distinguished by scholarship and other achievements' in the Muslim world.[41] Some Azharis had the *nisba al-Daghistani* (or *al-Daghusta-
ni*) or *al-Sharkasi* (Circassian), showing their Caucasian origin. The intensive cultural exchange between the pre-modern centres of Islamic knowledge in the northern Caucasus and
the Middle East resulted in the importation of Arabic manuscripts into the northern Caucasus. These circulated in numerous copies made in local *madrasa*s in the fifteenth–nineteenth centuries. In Daghestan alone there were over 400 private, mosque and state collections of Arabic manuscripts dating from the twelfth to the twentieth centuries, the majority of which have been preserved to modern times.[42]

Muslim students from the Caucasus used to continue their Islamic education in universities of the Middle East.[43] There were renowned visiting professors among the Daghestani scholars, like the lawyer Muhammad ibn Musa al-Quduqi (from the Avar village

of Qudutl), invited to work at al-Azhar by an Ottoman *şeyhül İslam* of the mid-seventeenth century. Later he practised in Muslim courts of the Hijaz and Yemen, where he became a disciple of the famous *mujtahid* Salih al-Yamani (d. 1697).[44] The mastery of traditional Islamic sciences (Ar. *'ulum al-din*) among the Daghestani scholars was very high and those who met them were impressed by their command of the Arabic language and Islamic knowledge. The eminent Yemeni *'alim* of the late eighteenth–early nineteenth centuries, Ahmad al-Shawqani reflected:

> I have not seen anyone equal to him [a Daghestani scholar — V.B.] in expressiveness and the use of the Arabic language in its totality. Indeed he was an eloquent man. And he had a good accent and his speech flowed pleasantly so that when I listened to him I was utterly inspired.[45]

It is these long-lasting cultural contacts that are in all likelihood reflected in a story of an army of Arab warriors wandering in the Arab Middle East and Iran before the appearance of the legendary Abu Muslim and his arrival in the Caucasus to proselytize the ignorant infidel (Ar. *jahilun*) highlanders. This narrative has not yet attracted the attention of scholars. It is reported in the *Ta'rikh Maza*, a popular Arabic chronicle which is known in hundreds of copies:

> You should know that the shaykh Sayyid Ahmad, shaykh Abu Ishaq Ibrahim and shaykh 'Ali, the descendants of Hamza, the uncle of the Prophet, peace be upon Him, as well as descendants of 'Abbas, another uncle of the Prophet, including the shaykh Muhammad and shaykh Nasir al-Din, accompanied by two thousand[46] men of their relatives, left noble Mecca and happy Medina in (sic) two hundred years after the Hijra.[47] They gained al-Sham [scil. Syria] and stayed there for several years. They left this land having just five thousand men and arrived in Misr [Egypt]. Staying there for some time they moved towards the land (Ar. nahiya) of Charkas [Circassia] not resting until they reached it. In those days these lands were the domain of war (Ar. dar al-harb). For this reason they undertook a raid (Ar. ghazw) and conducted the great holy war there...[48] Later they agreed to come to the country (Ar. wilaya) of Haydaq [Qaytaq — V.B.]...[49]

When one reads this passage, one may wonder why the Arab *ghazi*s took such a long and strange path from Mecca to Daghestan. First they moved straight to the north, towards Syria, then they turned towards Egypt in the south, then again to the north-east towards Iran, before reaching Circassian lands and coming back to the khanate of Qaytaq in central

Daghestan, where they decided to settle. The anonymous author of the *Ta'rikh Maza* dates these wanderings to the second or the third century AH (8th–early 9th centuries), when all the countries mentioned in it were under Islamic rule as integral parts of the Arab caliphate. I propose to seek an explanation of this passage rather in the cultural memory of the north Caucasian Muslims than in their real historical past. In this respect one may compare the itinerary of the Arab *ghazis* with wanderings of Muslim students and scholars from the Caucasus and Muslim areas close by in search of Islamic knowledge. Indeed, these students and scholars used to move quite easily between *madrasas* and universities of Daghestan, Syria, Egypt, Hijaz and Yemen. A permanent educational movement which connected these areas had neither a clear direction nor a proposed end.[50] It is noteworthy that there was a distinct impact of the Shafi'i legal school in all these Middle Eastern countries. From the twelfth century onwards the Shafi'i *madhhab* dominated the north-eastern Caucasus as well.

THE SHI'I INFLUENCES ON THE CULT OF ABU MUSLIM

Apart from the Arab East, the medieval North Caucasus maintained close links with Iran, dating back at least to the Sasanid period. From what early Arab geographers tell us, it emerges that even at the beginning of the second stage of the islamization of the Caucasus, the people of Zerihgheran (the ancient Iranian name of the village at present known as Kubachi) practised Zoroastrianism, introduced into Daghestan from pre-Islamic Iran a long time before.[51] The *Derbend-nameh* and *Akhty-nameh* retained the memory of Sasanid kings who settled Jews and northern Iranian tribes in the territory of contemporary Azerbaijan and southern Daghestan. The anonymous author of *Ta'rikh Abi Muslim* called both real early medieval Arab rulers and imaginary descendants of Abu Muslim by Iranian titles (Ir. *shah, shirvan-shah, mihtar*).[52] Pre-Islamic ties between the northern Caucasus and Iran were also reflected in a legend of Iskhak Kundishkan, the Jewish ruler of Akhty, who is reported to have been married to the sister of Abu Muslim. According to another version of this legend, her husband was Darwishaya, a descendant of Iranian warriors who founded the village of Akhty under the rule of the famous pre-Islamic Sasanid king Khosrov I Anushirvan.[53] With the development of Muslim society, these political and religious ties persisted, but acquired a more and more marked Islamic character.

Starting from the early Islamic period the northern Caucasus also developed cultural and religious ties with Central Asia. The cult of Abu Muslim sheds light on the nature of these links. One can find distinct parallels between historical narratives and religious practices associated with this *shaykh* in both areas. Like Daghestanis, local Muslims regard him as an agent of their islamization. A great many Central Asian mausoleums and holy places were ascribed to Abu Muslim, for example those near the town of Khorezm in Uzbekistan.[54] It is significant that both regions experienced strong cultural and religious influences from Iran. We may guess that *Abu Muslim-nameh* and other Iranian popular poetry and tales (Ar./Pers. *qisas*), which were widespread in both the Caucasus and Central Asia from the late eighth century, played an important role in the development of a historical legend about Abu Muslim.[55] As far as the Iranian Muslim influence is concerned, this had a distinct Shi'i character. In the 8th–12th centuries Shi'ism was extremely popular among the Muslim peoples of Iran, Central Asia and the Caucasus. Recent anthropological studies on the Central Asian holy places have revealed that dissident Shi'i notions are likely to have influenced religious practices related to the early Muslim saints, and especially 'Ali ibn Abi Talib and Abu Muslim.[56]

Though the cult of Abu Muslim had a distinct Shi'i background in its early Iranian and Central Asian versions, it retained only a few Shi'i elements in Daghestan. Unlike the early Shi'i influences linked with different dissident groups including that of the Abu-Muslimiyya, in Daghestan the Shi'i ideas of the cult of Abu Muslim related to the Imamiyya (Twelver Shi'a) branch in its Safavi version. Apparently, there was a Shi'i note in the introduction (Ar. '*unwan*) of *Ta'rikh Abi Muslim* informing us that the father of the *shaykh* was a *shahid* 'fighting for Husayn ibn 'Ali', the third Shi'i *imam*. There was also the 16th-century Shi'i version of *Ta'rikh Daghistan* revised by 'Abd al-Rahim al-Shirvani al-Husayni al-'Alawi al-Safawi, the *qadi* of Ghazi-Ghumuq, whose *laqab* "'Alawi" points to his Shi'i identity. In some late versions of this famous chronicle the names of Muhammad Mulla-Rafi' and 'Abd al-Rahim al-Shirwani were made to overlap, with the result that a Safavi descent was invented for the author of *Ta'rikh Daghistan*.[57] Shi'i inscriptions of the 16th century can be found on Abu Muslim's dress (Ar. *khirqa*) kept in his *ziyara* in Qhunzaqh. These include typical praises of 'Ali ibn Abi Talib and devout appeals to the Twelve *imam*s written in black, red and green ink in Arabic and Persian.[58]

Why such a difference? I suggest that a gradual transformation in the image of the Shi'a among the Daghestani Muslims was due to the late proselytizing activities of the Safavid rulers of Iran in the northern Caucasus in the 16th–18th centuries, attested by the Shi'i versions of the Daghestani chronicles and new Shi'i reliquaries in local holy places. During the first two stages of islamization people's minds were quite favourable to different dissident branches of the Shi'a as the introduction of *Ta'rikh Abi Muslim* hints. In the third stage of the islamization the Safavids undertook a wide military expansion in Derbend and Highland Daghestan. But the Shi'is failed to strike deep roots anywhere in the area apart from a small Shi'i community in Derbend and in the southern Daghestani villages of Miskinja and Qurush, where Shi'is from Iran were resettled. The majority of Daghestani Muslims remained Sunnis rigorously opposed to the Shi'a. This can be illustrated by a legend of Shi'i flavour concerning Abu Muslim. There are ruins of an Iranian fortress built during the Safavid expansion near the Tabasaran village of Khuchni in southern Daghestan. The place is known as the "fortress of seven brothers" (Az. *Eddi kardash qalası*). The legend ascribes it to seven giant brother-goblins (*nart*s), keepers of the miraculous sword of Abu Muslim. They used to terrorize neighbouring villages until the highlanders aroused themselves and killed them.[59] Only under Soviet rule did confrontations between Caucasian Shi'is and Sunnis die out.

ISLAMIC TRANSFORMATION OF PRE-MUSLIM HOLY PLACES

The cult of Abu Muslim is also very relevant for a re-consideration of the nature of religious syncretism in the northern Caucasian context. There is a widespread and rather misleading notion of the persistence of archaic pagan cults within Islam. In reality, Islam had to compete in the region not only with pagan beliefs but also with Zoroastrianism, Judaism (on the territory of Daghestan and Chechnya) and especially Christianity in its Orthodox version. The ousting of Christianity and other religions by Islam was a gradual and lengthy process which is reflected in written sources and oral ethnographic tradition. Some pre-Islamic beliefs and practices were retained by North Caucasian Muslims. But all of them were gradually rethought via adaptation to Islamic religious practices in a local social context. Religious practices associated with Abu Muslim confirm my argument. Of course, many holy places ascribed to this *shaykh* saint emerged a long time before the advent of Islam in the Caucasus. I refer here especially to veneration of stones and plants, as well as to some agrarian rituals.

Among ethnographic materials showing an Islamic re-interpretation of local pagan-mono-theistic beliefs, I would like to draw attention to the veneration of weapons.

It is noteworthy that there were three *ziyarat*s of the sword of Abu Muslim in Highland Daghestan alone. The oldest holy place is located on the outskirts of the Tabasaran village of Churdaf. It is called *Turil Yishv* (Tab. "The place of the sword"). Its presence is confirmed in the records of Muslim travellers and geographers from the early 12th century. Initially the holy place was associated with Maslama, the real conqueror of southern Daghestan, as the famous Arab writer Abu Hamid al-Gharnati al-Andalusi (1080–1169 AD) reported:

> Having settled twenty four thousand families [Ar. buyut] from the Arabs of Mosul, Damas-cus, Hims, Tadmur, Halab and other lands in Syria and Iraq, [Maslama] decided to leave [them], but Tabarsarlans [i.e. Tabasarans — V.B.] appealed to him: 'We fear that when you abandon us, O amir, these peoples [infidel highlanders recently converted to Islam — V.B.] might apostatize and we will be damaged from their neighbourhood again.' Then Maslama untied his sword and said: 'Let my sword be among you. Put it here. While it is here, among you, no one of these peoples will break their faith.[60]

Zakariya' al-Qazwini (ca. 1203–1283) provides the evidence of gradual changes as they occurred in the sanctuary almost one hundred years after the record of al-Gharnati. On the one hand, the main pre-Islamic beliefs and rituals were preserved. For instance, it was pro-hibited to enter the shrine in coloured dress, in order not to cause offence to a deity of the place living in the sword. On the other hand, a mosque was built on the holy site. The no-tion of the sacred is associated with the Muslim house of worship as such:

> Outside the town of Derbend there is a hill. A mosque is built on it with a sword kept in its prayer niche (Ar. mihrab). It is said to have belonged to Maslama ibn 'Abd al-Ma-lik ibn Marwan. The pilgrims visit it in white clothes only. If anybody approaches it in col-oured clothes, heavy rain falls and a strong wind arises killing everyone in the environs of the hill.[61]

In the course of islamization the pagan beliefs of the sanctuary declined, some of its rit-uals being preserved in a modified form. The 15th-century Arab geographer, Abu 'Abdallah Muhammad al-Himyari, described how the people from Derbend and neighbouring high-land villages performed regular pilgrimages to the holy place. In spring and at the beginning of autumn they drew the sword out of its old habit and gave it a new one. After the harvest pilgrims scattered grains in the mosque and throughout the hill. Since the territory of the sanctuary is believed to be sacred no one was allowed to take from its plants and fruits or to persecute criminals inside it. By this time the sanctuary was associated with Abu Muslim.[62] The 17th-century Ottoman traveller Evliya Çelebi recorded the existence of a new mosque or house of worship in *Turil Yishv*. He saw neither beliefs associated with the colour of dress of pilgrims, nor the ritual of "dressing the sword". Instead people used to gather in this *ziyara* during Qurban-Bayram and other great Muslim feasts and distribute the alms (Ar. *sadaqa*) collected there.[63] By the 19th century the sanctuary had moved from the mountain to the outskirts of Churdaf where it is located at present. A legend recorded in 1890 reports that the sword was then hidden in the house of a 19th-century *ghazi*. Once a year elders of the village performed a pilgrimage to the sword. No one was allowed to touch it. Otherwise a great war might begin.[64] Nowadays the holy place is still functioning, but in typical Muslim manner and without the sword.

The history of Abu Muslim's sword venerated in Churdaf is relevant for our understanding of the real relationship between continuity and change in pre-Islamic beliefs and practices among the North Caucasian Muslims. These inevitably change in the Muslim context, but they preserve their basic functions. Thus the veneration of weapons is always linked with agrarian rituals ensuring the fertility of the land.[65] This is how it functioned in the holy place of Churdaf. So did holy places of Abu Muslim in the Avar villages of Qhunzaqh and Chokh, also places where his swords were kept. During the spring festival 'of the first Furrow' (Av. *ots bay*) the chief of a clan claiming to be the descendants of this *shaykh* took part in a ceremony holding a sword in his hand.[66] The Tabasaran rock *Dajdin likar* (Tab. "Donkey's legs") also associated with Abu Muslim's weapons was used to pray for rain. To get rain people pour water into a hole which is said to have been pierced by the pick of Abu Muslim.[67] On the other hand, after islamization holy places reflect not a pagan pantheon or pagan-Islamic synthesis, as is often thought, but the cult of Muslim saints. It is significant that their veneration is associated with militant Muslim warriors. The rites are performed not by pagan priests but by mosque *imam*s, *'ulama'* or Sufi *shaykh*s.

CONCLUSION

Let us summarize our argument. This article is about the relationship between reality and fiction, continuity and change in the centuries-long islamization of the North Caucasus. It looks in particular at the image of Abu Muslim, a saint *shaykh* who is deemed to have diffused Islam throughout this area. From chronicles and oral histories it may be deduced that Abu Muslim is a kind of 'collective actor' of the islamization of the area. I argue that his properties were derived from different Muslim missionaries of foreign and local origin. Reality and mythology are irrevocably mixed in him. Through the analysis of narratives, religious practices and oral histories associated with Abu Muslim it is possible to reconsider a number of important problems, such as the principal periods and agents of islamization in this region, cultural and political links between the pre-modern North Caucasus, Central Asia, the Middle East and Iran, the Shi'i influence on late medieval Daghestan, and the Islamic transformation of pre-Muslim holy places.

ABBREVIATIONS

Av.	Avar
AN SSSR	Akademiia nauk SSSR [Academy of Sciences of the Soviet Union, today The Russian Academy of Sciences]
Ar.	Arabic
Az.	Azeri
Dag.	Nakh-Daghestani languages
DGU	Dagestanskii gosudarstvennyi universitet [Daghestani State University], Makhachkala
DNTs	Dagestanskii nauchnyi tsentr [Daghestani Scientific Centre of the Russian Academy of Sciences], Makhachkala
IEA	Institut etnologii i antropologii [Institute of Ethnology and Anthropology of the Russian Academy of Sciences], Moscow
IIAE	Institut istorii, arkheologii i etnografii [Institute of History, Archaeology and Ethnography], Makhachkala
IIIaL	Institut istorii, iazyka i literatury im. Gamzata Tsadasy [Gamzat Tsadasa Institute of History, Language and Literature, today Institute of History, Archaeology and Ethnography of the Daghestani Scientific Centre of the Russian Academy of Sciences], Makhachkala
Ir.	Iranian
IV	Institut vostokovedeniia [Institute for Oriental Studies], Moscow, St. Petersburg
KSIE	Kratkie soobshcheniia Instituta etnografii [Institute of Ethnology Newsletter], Moscow
OGIZ	Gosudarstvennoe sotsial'no-ekonomicheskoe izdatel'stvo [State Social Economic Publishing House], Moscow-Leningrad
Per.	Persian
RAN	Rossiiskaia akademiia nauk [The Russian Academy of Sciences]
RF	Rukopisnyi fond [Collection of manuscripts]
Rus.	Russian
Rut.	Rutul
SMOMPK	Sbornik materialov dlia opisaniia mestnostei i plemen Kavkaza [Collected materials for the description of areas and peoples in the Caucasus], Tiflis

SSKG   Sbornik svedenii o kavkazskikh gortsakh [Collected materials relating to the Caucasian
            highlanders], Tiflis
Tab.   Tabasaran
Turk.   Turkish

NOTES

1   For an extended Russian version see Vladimir O. Bobrovnikov and Ruslan I. Seferbekov, 'Abu Muslim i
      musul'man Vostochnogo Kavkaza: k istorii i etnografii Kul'tov sviatykh', in: Sergei N. Abashin and Vladimir
      O. Bobrovnikov (eds.), *Podvizhniki Islama: Kul't sviatyk i sufizm v Srednei Azii i na Kavkaze* (Moscow,
      2003), pp. 154-214.
2   'Darband-nama', in A.R. Shikhsaidov, T. M. Aitberov, G. M.-R. Orazaev (eds.), *Dagestanskie istoricheskie
      sochineniia* (Moscow, 1993), pp. 24-7, 32-5. Cf. 'Akhty-nama', 'Ta'rikh Abi Muslim', 'Ta'rikh Daghistan',
      ibid., pp. 69-72, 80-81, 99-104; 'Daghistan busurmantliyatlul istoriya', in T.M. Aitberov (comp. and ed.),
      Khrestomatiia po istorii prava i gosudarstva Dagestana v XVIII — XIX vv. (Makhachkala, 1999), Pt. 2, pp.
      23-4.
3   According to another version of this legend, Umm al-Mu'minat was the *shaykh*'s daughter – V.O. Bobrovnikov,
      'Abu Muslim', in S.M. Prozorov (ed.), *Islam na territorii byvshei Rossiyskoi imperii. Entsiklopedicheskii slovar'*
      (Moscow, 1999), fasc. 2, p. 6. Cf. 'Akhty-nama', pp. 69-72; 'Ta'rikh Abi Muslim', p. 80. The popular
      explanation of the meaning of the word Akhty cited above is wrong. The word Akhty has a local Lezgin
      origin.
4   L.I. Lavrov (coll. and ed.), *Epigraficheskie pamiatniki Severnogo Kavkaza*, Pt. 3, X — XX vv. (Moscow,
      1980), p. 87.
5   The inscription is reported to have been copied by a Muslim scholar from Richa from the ancient village
      chronicle following the restoration of the mosque in 1961. Quoted from the field materials of Amri
      Shikhsaidov published in his book *Islam v srednevekovom Dagestane, VII — XV vv.* (Makhachkala, 1969),
      p. 96.
6   'Abbas Quli Agha Bakikhanov, *Gulistan-i Iram* (Baku, 1991), pp. 55-8; Hasan Efendi al-Alqadari, *Athar-i
      Daghistan* (Makhachkala, 1994), p. 20.
7   N.V. Khanykov, 'Ocherk uchenoi deiatel'nosti za Kavkazom v 1850 g.', *Kavkaz* (Tiflis), 1851, No. 26.
8   M.-S. Saidov, 'O rasprostranenii Abu Muslimom islama v Dagestane', *Uchenye zapiski IIIaL* (Makhachkala),
      1957, Vol. 2, pp. 42-51; V.F. Minorskii, *Istoriia Shirvana i Derbenta X — XI vv.* (Moscow, 1963), pp. 24-
      5; A.R. Shikhsaidov, *Islam v srednevekovom Dagestane...*, pp. 58, 67, 88-112; A.E. Krishtopa, 'K voprosu
      o pis'mennykh istochnikakh po periodu feodalizma v Dagestane', *Voprosy istorii i etnografii Dagestana*
      (Makhachkala), issue 1, pp. 150-1; T.M. Aitberov, *Drevnii Khunzakh i khunzakhtsy* (Makhachkala, 1990),
      pp. 21, 36, 68-75. For an account of other works concerning the narratives of Abu Muslim see Bobrovnikov,
      'Abu Muslim', pp. 7-8.
9   Such an approach was initiated by Minorsky in his *Istoriia Shirvana i Derbenta X — XI vv.*, pp. 24-5.
10   See M. Halbwachs, *La mémoire collective* (Paris, 1969); Jan Assmann, *Das kulturelle Gedächtnis. Schrift,
      Erinnerung und politische Identität in frühen Hochkulturen* (Munich, 1992), pp. 17, 48.
11   Ibid., p. 77.
12   'Ta'rikh Daghistan', pp. 99-100, 102, 104.
13   'Min Ta'rikh Daghistan maktub bi-Inkachilaw', RF IIAE (Makhachkala), f. (collection) 1, op. (file) 1, d.
      (document) 378, p. 6b. Cf. 'Ta'rikh Maza', in *Dagestanskie istoricheskie sochineniia*, p. 115.
14   See for example, 'Ta'rikh Daghistan', p. 105; 'Ta'rikh Irhan', in *Dagestanskie istoricheskie sochineniia*, p.
      166. Versions of these chronicles written in the 19th century often call him Russian. This seems to be an
      anachronism that appeared under the influence of anti-colonial resistance by Caucasian Muslims against
      the Russian conquest.
15   This argument can be found in Alikber Alikberov, *Epokha Klassicheskogo islama na Kavkaze: Abu Bakr al-
      Darbandi i ego sufiiskaia entsiklopediia 'Raikhan al-Khakaik'* (Moscow, 2003). See also Bobrovnikov, 'Abu
      Muslim', p. 7. It is noteworthy that Hasan Efendi al-Alqadari follows al-Darbandi's argument in his book.
      See *Athar-i Daghistan*, p. 20.
16   V.O. Bobrovnikov, 'Dagestan', in S.M. Prozorov (ed.), *Islam na territorii byvshei Rossiiskoi imperii.
      Entsiklopedicheskii slovar*, (Moscow, 1998), fasc. 1, p. 31. For works that provide an accurate treatment
      of the periods of islamization in Daghestan see also A.R. Shikhsaidov's *Islam v srednevekovom Dagestane*,
      and id., 'Islam in Dagestan', in L. Jonson and M. Esenov (eds.), *Political Islam and Conflicts in Russia and
      Central Asia* (Stockholm, 1999), pp. 59-60.
17   See for instance, 'Darband-nama', pp. 21-31, 37; 'Akhty-nama', pp. 69-71.
18   It is interesting that in the earliest versions of 'Darband-nama', which constituted the core of the text

published by Mirza A. Kazem-beg, Maslama was not yet confused with Abu Muslim. See *Derbend-Nameh or the History of Derbent* (St. Petersburg, 1851; Arabic text with English translation), pp. 504-6, 543-6.

19   This was argued by the Leningrad anthropologist L. I. Lavrov, on the basis of data from Arabic manuscripts and epigraphic inscriptions from medieval Dagestan. See *Epigraficheskie pamiatniki Severnogo Kavkaza*, Pt. 1, *X — XVII vv.*, pp. 179, 187-8, 194, 197, 207.

20   'Ta'rikh Abi Muslim', pp. 81-3; 'Ta'rikh Daghistan', p. 100; 'Ta'rikh Maza', p. 140; 'Ta'rikh Tledok', in RF IIAE (Makhachkala), f. 1, op. 1, d. 531.

21   A.R. Shikhsaidov, *Islam v srednevekovom Dagestane*, pp. 95, 111, 154-5; G.F. Chursin, *Avary* (Makhachkala, 1995), p. 50. For the stories about Abu Muslim in Chechnya see V.P. Pozhidaev, *Gortsy Severnogo Kavkaza. Ingushi, Chechentsy, Khevsury, Kabardintsy. Kratkii istoriko-etnograficheskii ocherk* (Moscow-Leningrad, 1926), p. 17.

22   M.E. Shilling, *Malye narody Dagestana* (Moscow, 1993), pp. 63-5.

23   The role of local Sufis in the diffusion of Islam in the North Caucasus was disregarded until the end of the 1990s. This important issue is being reconsidered at the moment. For studies in this direction see A.K. Alikberov, 'Severnyi Kavkaz', in S.M. Prozorov (ed.), *Islam na territorii byvshei Rossiyskoi imperii. Entsiklopedicheskii slovar* (Moscow, 2000), fasc. 3 (in print).

24   The inscription was discovered by M.-S. Saidov and then published by Lavrov in *Epigraficheskie pamiatniki Severnogo Kavkaza*, Pt. 1, *X — XVII vv.*, pp. 63-4; 267; a photograph was published in A.R. Shikhsaidov, *Epigraficheskie pamiatniki Dagestana X — XVII vv. kak istoricheskii istochnik* (Moscow, 1984). At the moment the stone with this inscription is lost.

25   Minorskii, *op.cit.*, pp. 124-5, 163.

26   'Ta'rikh Amir-Qalandar ibn Sultan Haydar', in *Dagestanskie istoricheskie sochineniia*, p. 148.

27   See V.O. Bobrovnikov, 'Udzhaghabyr', in S.M. Prozorov (ed.), *Islam na territorii byvshei Rossiiskoi imperii. Entsiklopedicheskii slovar* (Moscow, 1999), fasc. 2, p. 90; id., 'Rodovye sviatilishcha rutul'tsev', in T.F. Sivertseva (ed.), *Dagestanskoe selo: voprosy identichnosti: na primere rutul'tsev* (Moscow, 1999), pp. 102, 106.

28   For instance, the Avar word *hansa*, and the Rutul notion of *ha'sa* ("stick") are derived from Arabic.

29   'Ta'rikh Daghistan', pp. 102, 104.

30   A.G. Przhetslavskii, 'Dagestan, ego nravy i obychai', *Vestnik Evropy* (St. Petersburg), 1867, vol. III, p. 150. See also M.E. Shilling, 'Iz istorii odnogo zemledel'cheskogo kul'ta', *KSIE* (Moscow), 1946, issue 1, pp. 32-4.

31   See *Dagestanskie istoricheskie sochineniia*, pp. 190-9; *Khrestomatiia po istorii prava i gosudarstva Dagestana v XVIII — XIX vv.*, Pt. 2, pp. 12-5.

32   See also materials published in Bobrovnikov, 'Abu Muslim', p. 6.

33   A.N. Genko, 'Arabskii iazyk i kavkazovedenie', *Trudy vtoroi sessii Assotsiatsii arabistov* (Moscow-Leningrad, 1941), pp. 85-93; M.G. Gadzhiev, O.M. Davudov, A.R. Shikhsaidov (eds.), *Istoriia Dagestana s drevneishih vremen do kontsa XV v.* (Makhachkala, 1996), p. 407.

34   See Minorskii, *op.cit.*, pp. 19, 46, 47, 65. Cf. 'Darband-name', p. 32.

35   Genko, *op.cit.*, p. 85. For works about the Arab settlers in pre-modern and modern Caucasus see also 'Araby v Dagestane', *Biblioteka dlia chteniia* (St. Petersburg), 1838, vol. 2; Z.M. Buniiatov, *Azerbaidzhan v VII — IX vv.* (Baku, 1965), pp. 176-9; Minorskii, *op.cit.*, p. 203; A.R. Shikhsaidov, *Islam v srednevekovom Dagestane*, pp. 92-4; N.G. Volkova, 'Araby na Kavkaze', *Sovetskaia etnografiia* (Moscow), 1983, No. 2, pp. 41-51.

36   'Ta'rikh Daghistan', p. 100; 'Ta'rikh Maza', p. 127. This explanation of the term *shamkhal* is a pure linguistic fiction, putting Arabic words in a genitive construction of the Lak language.

37   See *Istoriia Dagestana s drevneishih vremen do kontsa XV v.*, pp. 407-8.

38   Zakarija Ben Muhammad Ben Mahmud el-Cazwini's *Kosmographie* (Göttingen, 1848), Vol. 2, pp. 404-5.

39   Amri Shikhsaidov, 'Sammlungen arabischer Handschriften in Dagestan', in M. Kemper, A. von Kügelgen, D. Yermakov (eds.), *Muslim Culture in Russia and Central Asia from the 18th to the Early 20th Centuries* (Berlin, 1996), p. 299.

40   A.R. Shikhsaidov, 'Ahmad al-Iamani', in S.M. Prozorov (ed.) *Islam na territorii byvshei Rossiiskoi imperii. Entsiklopedicheskii slovar* (Moscow, 1999), fasc. 2, pp. 9-10; Nazir al-Durgili, 'Nuzhat al-adhhan fi tarajim 'ulama' Daghistan', in RF IIAE (Makhachkala), f. 30, op. 2, d. 10830, p. 9; *Epigraficheskie pamiatniki Severnogo Kavkaza*, Pt. 2, *XVIII — XX vv.*, pp. 107-8; T.M. Aitberov, 'Pis'mo saiiida Mahammeda Kazi-Kumukhskogo dzhamaatam Kazi-Kumukha, Kala-Kureisha i Zirikhgerana, i osobenno saiiidu Ahmadu Iamani, XV v.', *Pis'mennye pamiatniki Vostoka* (Moscow), 1979, pp. 4-8.

41   A.R. Shikhsaidov, 'Knizhnye kollektsii Dagestana', in A. Shikhsaidov, A. Isaev (eds.), *Rukopisnaia i pechatnaia kniga v Dagestane* (Makhachkala, 1991), pp. 18-20; cf. 'Abbas Quli Agha Bakikhanov, *Gulistan-i Iram*, p. 205.

42   A.R. Shikhsaidov, 'Otchet o vypolnenii proiekta No 308 "Arabskie rukopisnye kollektsii Dagestana"', (unpublished manuscript, Shikhsaidov's private collection, Makhachkala), p. 44.

43   For more materials about pre-modern and modern educational links between the Daghestani *madrasa*s and al-Azhar see V. Bobrovnikov, 'Al-Azhar and Shari'a Courts in the twentieth-century Caucasus', *Middle Eastern Studies*, Vol. 37, No. 4 (2001), pp. 1-29.

44   A.R. Shikhsaidov, 'al-Kuduqi', in S.M. Prozorov (ed.) *Islam na territorii byvshei Rossiiskoi imperii. Entsiklopedicheskii slovar* (Moscow, 1999), fasc. 2, pp. 51-2; M. Gaidarbekov, 'Khronologiia istorii Dagestana', in RF IIAE (Makhachkala), f. 3, op. 1, d. 236, vol. 9, p. 20.

45   Al-Shawqani, *al-Badr al-tali' bi-mahasin man ba'd al-qarn al-sabi'* (Cairo, 1348 AH [1929-30]), pp. 290-1. I. Iu. Krachkovski, *Nad arabskimi rukopisiami* (Moscow, Leningrad, 1946), pp. 134, 138.

46   According to some versions of 'Ta'rikh Maza', their number was 1000. See *Dagestanskie istoricheskie sochineniia*, p. 136, n. "v".

47   According to some versions of 'Ta'rikh Maza', it occurred "in one hundred years" or "in the year 200 AH" [815-16]. See *Dagestanskie istoricheskie sochineniia*, p. 136, n. "b".

48   According to a longer version of 'Ta'rikh Maza', which is comparatively rare, descendants of Hamza and 'Abbas also visited Shirvan in their wanderings: "They left [noble al-Sham] having just five thousand able warriors, and moved to Misr, where they did not stay long before leaving it for Shirvan". See *Dagestanskie istoricheskie sochineniia*, p. 115.

49   Ibid., p. 136.

50   I derive my argument partly from the description of a permanent and non-directed cultural movement in western European medieval society given by Marc Bloch in his *La société féodale* (Paris, 1961).

51   Ya'qubi's account, quoted from A.R. Shikhsaidov, *Islam v srednevekovom Dagestane*, p. 120.

52   See *Dagestanskie istoricheskie sochineniia*, p. 81. For the social meaning of the term *mihtar* see T.M. Aitberov, 'Iz sotsial'noi terminologii agul'tsev (mihtar)', in *Otraslevaia leksika dagestanskih iazykov* (Makhachkala, 1984), pp. 145-7.

53   'Darband-nama', pp. 17-21; 'Akhty-nama', pp. 70-2; 'Ta'rikh Abi Muslim', p. 80.

54   See A.G.P. Snesarev, *Khorezmskie legendy kak istochnik po istorii religioznykh kul'tov Srednei Azii* (Moscow, 1983).

55   I draw this argument from Barthold's hypothesis outlined in his article 'Abu Muslim' in V.V. Bartold, *Sochineniia* (Moscow, 1971), pp. 479-80. No one has yet carried out a textual comparison of 'Abu Muslim-nama' with 'Ta'rikh Abi Muslim' and other written and oral narratives from Daghestan.

56   See A.G.P. Snesarev, *op.cit.*, pp. 18-23; A.K. Muminov, 'Tsentral'naia Aziia', in S.M. Prozorov (ed.), *Islam na territorii byvshei Rossiiskoi imperii. Entsiklopedicheskii slovar* (Moscow, 1998), fasc. 1, pp. 102-4.

57   Krishtopa, *op.cit.*, pp. 150-1.

58   For Persian and Arabic texts written on the dress in Qhunzaqh, see M.-S. Saidov, *O rasprostranenii Abu Muslimom islama v Dagestane*, pp. 50-1.

59   D. Donoguev, 'Bylina o semi brat'iakh-nartakh i ikh sestre', *SMOMPK* (Tiflis), 1889, Vol. XXVI, Pt. 2, pp. 19-20; A.N. Genko, 'Arabskii iazyk i Kavkazovedenie', in *Trudy Ntoroi sessii asotsiatsii arabiistov, 19-23 oktiabria 1937* (Moscow and Leningrad, 1941), pp. 104-7.

60   Abu Hamid al-Gharnati, *Tuhfat al-albab wa-nuhbat al-a'jab*, with Russian translation by O.G. Bol'shakov and A.L. Mongait (Moscow, 1971), p. 61.

61   *Kosmographie*, p. 340.

62   Anatolii Genko, "Arabskii iazyk I Kavkazovedenie. Oznachenii arabskikh materialov dlia izucheniia istorii Kavkaza," in *Trudy Ntoroi sessii asotsiatsii arabiistov, 19-23 oktiabria 1937* (Moscow and Leningrad, 1941), p. 104.

63   Evliya Çelebi, *Kniga puteshestvii* (Moscow, 1979; 2nd ed.).

64   Hasan Efendi al-Alqadari, *Athar-i Daghistan*, pp. 40-7.

65   See J. Frazer, *The Golden Bough* (London, 1977).

66   O. Karanailov, 'Aul Chokh', *SMOMPK* (Tiflis), Vol. IV, Pt. 2 (1884), pp. 1-24; Chursin, *Avary*, pp. 15-6.

67   R.I. Seferbekov, *Agrarnye kul'ty tabasarantsev* (Makhachkala, 1995), p. 52.

THE POLITICAL HISTORY OF DAGHESTAN IN THE TENTH-FIFTEENTH CENTURIES

AMRI SHIKHSAIDOV

This paper does not deal with the political history of Daghestan in the 10th–15th centuries in the narrow sense, but rather with the internal and external environment in which islamization took place. The Arab campaigns had an enormous, sometimes even a decisive, influence on the totality of personal, family, civil and confessional rights. They promoted the emergence of new forms of land relations and the formation of the economic and ideological base, which guaranteed Islam its eventual victory over paganism. The Arab conquests and the struggle of the peoples of Daghestan to keep their independence form one of the most important features of the history of Daghestan in the early Middle Ages.[1]

As elsewhere, so too in Daghestan Islam endorsed ethnic, political and ideological consolidation. However, this process was a lengthy one: it lasted for almost a millennium and was clearly divided into two periods. The first period – from the mid-seventh century to the first half of the tenth – was associated with the Arabs and the Arab conquests. The second – from the second half of the tenth century to the sixteenth century – was a period of peaceful, independent development of the numerous Daghestani statelets and unions of village communities.

This second period was characterized by a number of political, economic and ideological particularities, which coexisted with and "corrected" the process of islamization in the North-Eastern Caucasus. First among these was the ethnic division of the land. Abu Hamid al-Gharnati, the Arab traveler, historian and jurist, described it best: in 1131, while in Derbend, he saw the *amir* of that city, who read to the members of the *majlis* a work on *fiqh* by the Arab theologian Abu al-Hasan Ahmad al-Mahamili (978–1024). The *amir* then proceeded to comment on the book. According to al-Gharnati, he spoke in various languages, such as Lakan, Tabalan, Filan, Za'qalan, Khaydaq, Ghumiq, Sarir, Alan, Ass, Zerehgeran, Turkish, Arabic, Persian [...] He explained the contents [of the book] to each people in their own language.[2]

The description is crystal clear: Derbend was a multi-ethnic city, where members of all the various Daghestani peoples lived, and more importantly formed part of the Muslim community together with Arabs, Turks and Persians.[3] In fact, the islamization of many peoples began with the conversion of those of them who had settled in Derbend.

Indeed, during the first and the beginning of the second periods of islamization Derbend grew into the principal ideological and religious centre of Islam in the Caucasus and became the main springboard for the dissemination of the ideas of Islam and Arab-Islamic culture all over the northern Caucasus. This was best symbolized in the erection of the grandiose Friday [*Jum'a*] Mosque as early as the beginning of the eighth century. According to the Daghestani chronicle *Derbend Nameh*, the city had by then become completely Muslim, and in 115/733–34 the Arab general Maslama ordered the building of the Friday Mosque as well as of seven district mosques – one for each district of the city, each one inhabited by a different "tribe".[4]

More concretely, even during the first period of islamization, though the Arabs were the first and the main bearers of the ideas of Islam, they were not the only ethnic and social stratum actively promoting islamization. Al-Ya'qubi (d. 897) gives us the first news of the numerous Arab colonists settled in the middle of the eighth century in communities around Derbend. These Arab settlements had quickly grown into "Islamic centres" (*marakiz*).[5] Soon, however, certain strata of the local population came to play an important role in this process as well. Derbend, for example, was full of *ghazis*,[6] many of whom came from de-classified native elements.

By the end of the first period – in the early tenth century – Islam had gained strong positions in many areas adjacent to the Arab settlements around Derbend. This is especially true of Lakz, Tabasaran, Khaydaq and Urkarakh. The epigraphic monuments testify to an intensive process of construction of Muslim places of worship, especially in southern Daghestan (the mosques in Kara-Kura, Kochkhura and Fit-h, for example, were built in the tenth century).

In toto, however, three hundred years after the arrival of the first Muslims the embrace of the new religion was not universal. It was limited to the Caspian coastal strip from Derbend up to Semender; to southern Daghestan, including Tabasaran and the lands up to the middle Samur and Chirakhchay; and to part of the lands of the Darghins up to Urkarakh inclusive. Most of Daghestan remained pagan while in some parts of the country Christianity enjoyed a strong position. However, a powerful and solid base had already been established for the subsequent diffusion of Islam.

Furthermore, the events of the eleventh–fifteenth centuries would favourably affect the expansion of Islam in all of Daghestan.[7] Externally, large masses of other ethnic groups invaded Daghestan (the Kypchaks, the Seljuks, the Mongols, the troops of Timur) during the eleventh–fourteenth centuries. All of these were either Muslim or (like the Mongols) supported Islam and the *'ulama'*. These favourable external circumstances are one distinctive feature of the process of islamization in Daghestan.

Another, internal feature was the country's political geography in the tenth-fifteenth centuries. Just as in earlier times, Daghestan did not enjoy administrative-political unity in this period either. Administrative-political identity was divided among Lakz, Derbend, Ghumuq, Sarir, Zerehgeran, Khaydaq, Tabasaran and several dozen unions of village communities.[8] In view of the consolidating role of Islam it looks strange indeed that religious-ideological unity was not followed by unity in the administrative-political sphere too. However, the political culture which had developed over the centuries, together with the large number and variety of the individual polities, proved a fairly resilient factor countering such a development.

True, over this long period of time significant changes had occurred: some polities had declined (Lakz, Tabasaran, Zerehgeran, Sarir); others had grown stronger and expanded (Derbend, Ghumuq, Khaydaq). New unions of village communities stood out; and super-unions had formed. Yet in the simultaneous decline of some state structures and the growth of others, uneven development had been a normal phenomenon. Furthermore, it was precisely in this period (of the eleventh–fifteenth centuries) that mono-ethnic polities were replaced by multi-ethnic ones. Derbend, international already in the tenth century and perhaps even earlier, took the lead, to be followed by Ghumuq (the Shamkhalate of Ghazi Ghumuq) and Khaydaq (the Utsmiate of Qaytaq). Multi-ethnic feudal principalities had become a fairly frequent, almost normal phenomenon in Daghestan. Nevertheless, Daghestan remained divided into a large number of independent polities well into the future – until the Russian conquest in the mid-nineteenth century.

What is special about Daghestan is that despite the lack of unified political structures the unity of the country was nonetheless gradually advancing. The replacement of confessional pluralism by a single religion, Islam, facilitated this process very greatly. The interests of the

Daghestani principalities in their relations with the outside world overwhelmingly coincided, while the struggle for independence reinforced this political unity. This became apparent in the fourteenth–fifteenth centuries and was demonstrated visibly in the course of the devastating campaigns of the Mongols and Timur.

The accelerated pace of the islamization of Daghestan coincided chronologically with three important developments in Daghestani society. More precisely expressed, during the tenth–fifteenth centuries four inter-related and parallel processes took place, which defined the entire course of social, economic and political developments for centuries to come. These were: (1) the complete islamization of Daghestan; (2) the strengthening of the institution of the rural community; (3) the formation of capital settlements; and (4) the forging of overall economic unity.

The village community made a huge imprint on the course and the degree of development of Daghestani society in the tenth–fifteenth centuries. It played a double role in the social development of Daghestan. On the one hand it defended the rights of the peasants and established a level of taxes and duties. On the other hand a community which had become dependent on a feudal principality became a fiscal unit guaranteeing a regular tax income. These circumstances defined both Daghestan's slow pace of feudalization and the centuries-long stability of the community.

The stability of the village community accelerated the process of formation of capital settlements.[9] This was a lengthy process lasting several centuries (mainly tenth–fifteenth centuries), which had several variations. The most common of these was the relocation of several small settlements to a single central one, which would become a capital settlement, however, only after the further relocation into it of several more middle size settlements. The relocation itself was not always a single move, but might last over two to three centuries. This variation did not create a new settlement but strengthened an existing one territorially. As for the mechanism of relocation itself, it also had several variations. In the commonest pattern, each component settlement retained its own character, structure and probably status within the new one. Each previously independent settlement occupied a quarter of its own within the new one, which usually coincided with the territory of a single *tukhum* (clan). The number of quarters and *tukhum*s in a capital settlement was usually identical.[10]

The formation of capital settlements was the leading process in Daghestan, but it was not the only one. A parallel process of disintegration of capital settlements took place as well, especially in areas which became battle zones. In addition, in many areas, especially in the western parts of Daghestan, the formation of capital settlements never took place at all.[11]

All of this resulted in a cardinal change, the emergence of the political centres of the Daghestani principalities and unions of village communities. Places like Akhty, Richa, Tsakhur, Rutul, Tbigh, Khuchni, Khif, Aqusha, Tsudaqar, Qhunzakh, Ghumuq, Tsoghratl, Mugi, Meheb, Endirey, Bishta, Qoroda, Chokh, Targhi, Gubdan, Qadar, Karata, Meqkhelta, Qahib, Harkas, Hutsatl, Balqar, Oboda, Qubachi, and others, became political, administrative, cultural, ideological and economic centres of micro-regions. Such a combination of functions and activity makes them equivalent to medieval cities. The emergence of a great number of such capital settlements playing the role of cities is a development unique to medieval Daghestan. These capital settlements developed into "Islamic centres" with significant activity in education and Arabic book culture.

The most important development accompanying the "compact islamization" of Daghestan was the economic unification of Daghestan. Geography and ecology defined the main directions and characteristics of economic activity. The high alpine areas were oriented towards animal husbandry; the lower mountain and foothill areas towards agriculture, animal husbandry (mainly sheep and goats) and home industry; the plains towards the growing of grain, gardening and cattle husbandry.[12] The orientation of the different geographic zones towards different branches of economic activity, with varying degrees of intensity, stimulated lasting and stable economic contacts. Yet until the beginning of the tenth century these were systematically interrupted. The campaigns of the Huns, the Savirs, the Khazars, and the Arabs transformed the plains into a zone of war and stopped their development into an area of agricultural activity.

These circumstances changed drastically in the tenth century. From then until the beginning of the thirteenth century, during a period of more than two hundred years, the most important process was the maintenance of peaceful contacts between the plains and the mountains. Even the Mongol conquests and Timur's campaigns were unable to reverse this course of events. The plains had become the breadbasket of Daghestan. Accordingly the mountain regions remained firmly fixed on their traditional economy. The economic unity of Daghestan, which developed under these conditions of stability in the plains-mountains inter-relationship between the tenth and the fifteenth centuries, became the basis for political unity. The maintenance of stability, the good-neighbourly relations of the Daghestani states and unions of rural communities, and the general orientation towards peace together provided for a sound economic basis and economic stimuli in the country as a whole.

Thus, all these processes – the strengthening of rural communities, the emergence of capital settlements performing the functions of cities, the unification of the political interests of the various states and unions of village communities, the single economic microstructure and a single confessional system – merged into a knot of inter-connected and inter-dependent factors, influenced overall by the generally peaceful situation from the tenth to the fifteenth centuries.

The concluding phase of islamization also had a distinctive character.[13] First of all, the main agents of islamization were now not the Arabs, but other ethnic groups: Daghestani *ghazi*s based in Derbend; the various Daghestani capitals which had converted to Islam and were spreading that faith into neighbouring areas (Karakura, Tsakhur, Qal'a-Qoreysh, Ghumukq-Ghazighumuq and others); Shirvan and its offshoots in Daghestan; and Turks (the Kypchaks, the Seljuks, the Turkic majority in the Mongol armies, Timur and the Safavids).

The role of the Daghestani political centres can be understood from the example of Kumukh, the capital of the Ghumukq Shamkhalate, which after its conversion to Islam (most probably in the second half of the fourteenth century) was renamed Ghazighumukq. According to Timur's historian, Nizam al-Din Shami, "the district of Kazikumukluk and the armies of Awkhar have a habit of fighting the unbelievers each year and month".[14] It was particularly to "wilayat Kumukh" that Ahmad al-Yamani was sent from Egypt in the 1420s "by order of the *khalifa* of God's messenger" to propagate Islam and the (religious) sciences.[15]

Secondly, the forms and methods of islamization also changed. Military campaigning and the use of force were replaced by massive proselytizing activity and economic forms of pressure. Sufism became the main form of Islam in Daghestan. In the tenth–twelfth centuries Derbend turned into an important centre for Sufis and for Sufi practice. The existing Arab settlements, which had developed into Islamic centres, also developed into centres of Sufi learning and practice, that is into *ribat*s. This helps to make clear the status and role of the *ghazi*s inhabiting these centres in the process of islamization[16] as well as the mechanism of islamization itself: it proceeded within the broad confines of Sufism.[17]

Usually in the Middle East the centres of Sufi ideas were the cities. In Daghestan this meant Derbend. However, in Daghestan during the last thousand years Sufism has found a home also in rural areas, especially in the centres of political structures (such as the villages of Tpigh, Meshlesh, Orta-Stal, Akhty, Khnof, Gelkhan and others). One thing pointing to the wide diffusion of Sufism in Daghestan is the numerous holy places (*pirs*, or *ziyarat*s) which have survived and are especially esteemed by the local population and are connected particularly to Sufis: Orta-Stal (twelfth–thirteenth centuries and sixteenth century), Khnof (beginning of the fifteenth century), Khuri (fifteenth century), Gelkhan (sixteenth century), Tpigh (seventeenth century). These monuments of religious architecture have still not been studied at all.

Another testimony to this is the great number of copies of books by al-Ghazali – *Ihya' 'Ulum al-Din, Minhaj al-'Abidin, Jawahir al-Qur'an, al-Wajiz, Bidayat al-Hidaya* – copied between 1191 and the end of the seventeenth century that have been found in Daghestan.[18] More than thirty are known. All of these (with the exception of a single one written in 1191), were copied in the fifteenth–seventeenth centuries in various villages in Daghestan: Shiri, Aqusha, Qubachi, Mugi, Itsari, Arakul, Tsada, Karata and others. There seems to have been a great deal of interest in Daghestan in al-Ghazali's works during these centuries.

The Shafi'i *madhhab* was the one that prevailed from the very beginning in Daghestan. The consolidation of the Shafi'i *madhhab* in Daghestan also determined the thematic and spiritual character of the scientific and educational literature imported from the countries of the Near and Middle East.[19] The great Muslim theologian and mystic, author of an encyclopedic dictionary of Sufi terms, *Rayhan al-Haqa'iq wa-Bustan al-Daqa'iq*, Abu Bakr Muhammad b. Musa (d. beginning of the twelfth century) was a Shafi'i,[20] as were the majority of the spiritual élite of Derbend. As was noted earlier, in 1131 the Andalusi traveler and historian, Abu Hamid al-Gharnati, himself a Shafi'i, read in the *majlis* of Derbend the juristic tract of Abu al-Hasan Ahmad al-Mahamili, a Shafi'i theologian from Baghdad.[21] According to Zakariya' al-Qazwini (d. 1283), two popular works by Shafi'i *fuqaha'* were translated in the famous *madrasa* (established by Nizam al-Mulk in 1075) of the village of Tsakhur into the "Lakz" language. Qazwini wrote about the residents of Tsakhur that they had

> a khatib who prays together with them and a qadi who rules on their disputes according to the teaching of al-Shafi'i. All the residents of the city are Shafi'is.22

The famous Arab traveler Ibn Battuta (1304-1377) mentions the arrival in Saray-Berke of a "Shafi'i *mudarris*" from Daghestan, the *faqih* Sadr al-Din Sulayman al-Lakzi.[23] Timur, on his arrival in Daghestan in 1396, gave the ruler he nominated over a Darghin settlement a treatise in Shafi'i law, so that he ruled "impartially and according to justice".[24]

The islamization of Daghestan in the tenth–fifteenth centuries proceeded under favourable external circumstances. This is especially true of the period from the tenth to the beginning of the thirteenth centuries. The revival of trade and economic ties with the cities of the Near East was accompanied by lasting and stable ties with the Arab-Islamic cultural world.

The presence of Daghestanis in the cities of the Near East and Central Asia was a normal phenomenon in the tenth–fifteenth centuries. Especially popular was Baghdad, until 1258 the capital of the caliphate and for centuries a major locus of scientific and cultural life. Many Daghestanis studied in the Nizamiyya *madrasa* in Baghdad and in similar institutions in other cities under the most famous teachers. Many of them afterwards became famous *fuqaha'* and engaged in teaching.

The incorporation of Daghestan into the sphere of the Arab-Islamic cultural tradition stimulated the importation of manuscripts from the centres of the Islamic world. Works in various sciences were brought over from Syria, Egypt, Iraq, Central Asia, Azerbaijan and other regions. Many of these works were copied by local *katib*s. This was especially true of the Qur'an, works on Arabic grammar, lexicography, Islamic law, logic, ethics, Sufism and exegesis. A new stage in the history of science and literature in Daghestan started with the advent of its own literary tradition, of the production there of original works in Arabic. The earliest examples of these can be assigned to the tenth century.[25]

NOTES

1   *Istoriia Dagestana* (Moscow, 1967), Vol. I; *Istoriia narodov Severnogo Kavkaza s drevneishikh vremen do kontsa XVIII v.* (Moscow, 1988); A. P. Novosel'tsev, *Khazarskoe gosudarstvo i ego rol' v istorii Vostochnoi Evropy i Kavkaza* (Moscow, 1990); A.R. Shikhsaidov, *Islam v srednevekovom Dagestane, VII-XV vv.* (Makhachkala, 1969).

2   O.G. Bol'shakov and A.L. Mongait (eds.), *Puteshestvie Abu Khamida al-Garnati v Vostochnuiu Evropu* (Moscow, 1971), p. 26.

3   The multi-ethnic character of the city can be glimpsed already in the tenth century, when the Arab author al-Istakhri (d. c. 951) wrote: "The residents of Bab al-Abwab use sometimes the Khazar language and the other languages of their mountains"; Istakhri, *al-Masalik wal-Mamalik*, re-edited by Muhammad Jabir 'Abd al-'Al al-Hini (Cairo, 1961), p. 113.

4   *Bibliotheca Geographorum Arabicorum*, VII, pp. 446-7; *Derbend Nameh*, translated from a select Turkish version and published by Mirza A. Kazem-Beg (St. Petersburg, 1851), p. 544.

5   M.J. de Goeje (ed.), *Annales quos scripsit Abu Djafar Mohammad b. Djarir at-Tabari,* Ser. II, Vol. I (Leyden, 1871), II, p. 1871.

6   V.F. Minorskii, *Istoriia Shirvana i Derbenda* (Moscow, 1961), pp. 46, 65, 70, 83, 124-5.

7   M.G. Gadzhiev, O.M. Davudov and A.R. Shikhsaidov, *Istoriia Dagestana* (Makhachkala, 1996), p. 226.

8   The village community (*sel'skaia obshchina* in Russian) was the basic polity in Daghestan. It included usually (but not always) a village and its hamlets. An alliance of village communities, or a "Society" (*obshchestvo* in Russian) was a permanent union of several village communities which formed a single ethnic-political entity. Only "Societies" and their confederations were entitled to engage in relations with other political units. For the village community, see M.A. Aglarov, *Sel'skaia obshchina v Nagornom Dagestane v XVII – nachale XIX v.* (Moscow, 1988; includes extensive bibliography). For the "Societies" and their alliances, see B.G. Aliev, *Soiuzy sel'skikh obshchestv Dagestana* (Makhachkala, 1999).

9   For the formation of capital settlements, see S.S. Agashirinova, "Poseleniia Lezgin v XIX – nachale XX v.", *Uchenye zapiski Instituta Istorii, Iazyka i Literatury* (Makhachkala, 1959); M.Z. Osmanov, "Poselenia Dargintsev v XIX – XX vv.", *Uchenye zapiski Instituta Istorii, Iazyka i Literatury* (Makhachkala, 1962); S.Sh. Gadzhieva, M.O. Osmanov and A.G. Pashaeva, *Material'naia kul'tura Dargintsev* (Makhachkala, 1965); A. Shikhsaidov, *Dagestan v X – XIV vv.* (Makhachkala, 1965).

10   Gadzhiev, Davudov and Shikhsaidov, *op.cit.*, pp. 265-8.

11   Ibid., p. 268.

12   Ibid., p. 233.

13   For Islam in Daghestan, see N. Khanikoff, 'Mémoire sur les inscriptions musulmanes du Caucase', *Journal Asiatique*, sér. 5, XX (1862), p. 214; 'Ali Ghumuqi, "Ala Yad man Aslamana', *Jaridat Daghestan*, 1918, No. 9; M.-S. Saidov, 'O raspostranenii Abumuslimom Islama v Dagestane', *Uchenye Zapiski Instituta Istorii, Iazyka i Literatury*, Vol. III (Makhachkala, 1956); Minorskii, *op.cit.* (includes extensive bibliography); Shikhsaidov, *Islam v Dagestane...*, *op.cit.*, (includes extensive bibliography); Sh.M. Akhmedov, 'K voprosu o raspostranenii Islama v Dagestane', *Voprosy Istorii Dagestana*, Vyp. 2 (Makhachkala, 1957); T.M. Aitberov, 'O raspostranenii Islama v Dagestane', *Bloknot agitatora i propagandista* (Makhachkala, 1988); A.K. Alikberov,'"Raikhan al-Khakaik va bustan ad-dakaik" Mukhammada ad-Darbandi kak pamiatnik musul'manskoi istoriografii', (St. Petersburg, 1991; autoreferat of a dissertation); id., 'Bab al-abwab', *Islam. Entsiklopedicheskii slovar'*, Vol. II (Moscow, 1999); V.O. Bobrovnikov, 'Abu Muslim', ibid.

14   B.G. Tizengauzen (ed.), *Sbornik materialov otnosiashchikhsia k istorii Zolotoi Ordy* (Moscow and Leningrad, 1941), II, p. 127.

15   A.R. Shikhsaidov, 'Akhmad al-Iamani', *Islam. Entsiklopedicheskii slovar'*, II, pp. 9-10.

16   Alikberov, *op.cit.* (dissertation), p. 12.

17   Ibid., *loc.cit.*

18   A.R. Shikhsaidov and A.B. Khalidov, 'Manuscripts of al-Ghazali's works in Daghestan', *Manuscripta Orientalia* (St. Petersburg), Vol. 3, No. 2 (June 1997).

19   In detail, see G.G. Gamzatov, M.-S. Saidov and A.R. Shikhsaidov, 'Arabo-musul'manskaia literaturnaia traditsiia v Dagestane', in G.G. Gamzatov (ed.), *Daghestan: istorizo-literaturnyi protses* (Makhachkala, 1990), pp. 211-246.

20   A.K. Alikberov, 'ad-Darbandi', *Islam. Entsiklopedicheskii slovar'*, II, pp. 33-4.

21   Bolshakov and Mongait (eds.), *op.cit.*, p. 26.

22   *Cazwini's Kosmographie*, II, p. 405; A.R. Shikhsaidov, 'Zakariia al-Kazvini v Dagestane', *Istochnikovedenie istorii dosovetskogo perioda* (Makhachkala, 1987), p. 100.

23   *Rihlat Ibn Battuta al-Musamma Tuhfat al-Nuzzar fi Ghara'ib al-Amsar wa-Aja'ib al-Asfar* (Beirut, 1985, 4th ed.), I, p. 394.

24   A.R. Shikhsaidov, 'Arkheograficheskaia rabota v Dagestane', *Izuchenie istorii i kul'tury Dagestana. Arkheograficheskii aspekt* (Makhachkala, 1988), p. 12.

25   M. Saidov, *Dagestanskaia literatura XVIII–XIX v. na arabskom iazyke* (Moscow, 1964); *Katalog arabskikh rukopisei Instituta Istorii, Iazyka i Literatury Dagestanskogo Filiala AN SSSR* (Moscow, 1977); G.G. Gamzatov, M.-S. Saidov and A.R. Shikhsaidov, 'Sokrovishnitsa pamiatnikov pis'mennosti', *Ezhegodnik Iberiisko-Kavkazskogo Iazykoznaniia* (Tbilisi, 1981); A.K. Alikberov, 'Raikhan al-khakaik', *Izuchenie istorii i kul'tury Dagestana. Sbornik stat'ei* (Makhachkala, 1988); Gadzhiev, Davudov and Shikhsaidov, *op.cit.*, pp. 408-16.

THE INTRODUCTION OF THE KHALIDIYYA AND THE QADIRIYYA INTO DAGHESTAN IN THE NINETEENTH CENTURY

MOSHE GAMMER

There is ample evidence of Sufis living and active in Daghestan through the centuries.[1] Nonetheless, it is only from the 1810s that Sufi orders were able to establish themselves in that country. This should not, perhaps, surprise. After all, the 12th/18th century witnessed great organizational and ideological changes in Sufism, which transformed many (though by no means all) *tariqa*s into what some scholars prefer to call *ta'ifa*s, while others dub this phenomenon "Neo-Sufism".[2] Thus, while until then Sufi Shaykhs had acted as individuals, the new *ta'ifa*s were centralized, disciplined organizations, with a clear chain of command. Being organizations they were also able, therefore, to continue their existence beyond the lifespan of a single person. Armed with both the old charisma of the Shaykh and the new tools of organization and ideology, the new *ta'ifa*s were able not only to establish themselves in new lands but also to become an integral part of their social fabric.

The two major Sufi brotherhoods which have since the nineteenth century been dominant in Daghestan – indeed in the Northern Caucasus as a whole – are the Naqshbandiyya (or rather the Naqshbandiyya-Mujaddidiyya-Khalidiyya, called "Miuridizm" by the Russian and Soviet sources) and the Qadiriyya (known as "Zikrizm" in Russian and Soviet literature).[3] The histories of these two *tariqa*s have for a long time been intertwined. Usually it was the Naqshbandiyya who arrived after the Qadiriyya and in many cases supplanted it. In the Caucasus, however, it was the Naqshbandiyya-Mujaddidiyya-Khalidiyya, which arrived first in the 1810s and 1820s.[4] Only some thirty years later did the Qadiriyya reach the northern Caucasus and in many places – mainly in Chechnya – replace the Naqshbandiyya.

The Naqshbandiyya, named after Shaykh Muhammad Baha' al-Din al-Naqshbandi (1318–1389), is one of the most dynamic, widespread and influential Sufi brotherhoods, mainly in the Eurasian parts of the Muslim world.[5] Shaykh Ahmad Faruqi Sirhindi (1564–1624) established the Mujaddidi branch of the Naqshbandiyya and thus transformed it into a *ta'ifa*. Furthermore, he transmuted the already "strictly orthodox"[6] brotherhood into "the vanguard of renascent Islamic orthodoxy".[7] Part of this "orthodoxy" has been the Naqshbandiyya's concern for the well-being of the *umma*, not merely the salvation of the individual. It has, thus, been interested – and indeed involved – in politics from an early stage.

The Khalidiyya is an autonomous sub-order of the Naqshbandiyya-Mujaddidiyya established by Shaykh Diya al-Din Khalid al-Shahrazuri (1776–1827).[8] Mawlana Khalid, as he is known to his followers, tightened the discipline and further strengthened the already centralized structure of his new sub-order. Moreover he infused it with zeal and drive, making it into the most active and dynamic branch of the Naqshbandiyya until the present.

The Qadiriyya, named after 'Abd al-Qadir al-Gilani (d. 1166), is probably the most widespread Sufi brotherhood, being present in practically all the countries of the Muslim world. Going back to a *qutb*, it is also one of the four most prestigious *tariqa*s.[9] Although no less "orthodox" than the Naqshbandiyya, the Qadiriyya is on the whole – a few exceptions on the periphery notwithstanding – a more "traditional" Sufi brotherhood interested mainly in the improvement of the individual and holding back from politics. Unlike the Naqshbandiyya, the Qadiriyya has not transformed itself into a *ta'ifa* – again there are a few exceptions – and its organization is highly diffused. Thus, while in principle the keeper of 'Abd al-Qadir's mausoleum in Baghdad (who is also a descendant of al-Gilani) is the supreme Shaykh of the *tariqa*, and all Qadiri Shaykhs acknowledge his authority and receive their *ijaza* from him, in practice each Shaykh enjoys complete independence and the *ijaza* is a mere formality.

While the order of arrival of these two *ta'ifa*s in Daghestan might be regarded as accidental, the almost immediate success of each in its turn cannot but be explained by the circumstances which they encountered on their arrival.

Daghestan, like the other parts of the Northern Caucasus, had since the 1770s been under the impact of Russian encroachment and conquest. This process undermined the traditional way of life and the political, economic and social structure of the entire country, both the parts under Russian rule and those which had not yet been conquered.

The economy of the "unpacified" parts of Daghestan was strongly affected by Russian economic warfare. Boycotts against specific communities and the prevention of others from using fields and winter pastures in the lowlands disrupted traditional patterns of commerce and food production upon which the highlanders were dependent for their survival. Russian "punitive expeditions", destroying everything in their path, further disrupted the economic life of these communities, while the thwarting of a great part of their raids – a traditional way to supplement their income – played its part as well.

The "pacified" parts of Daghestan did not fare better. Having already incurred the direct and indirect damage of the disruption of commerce, they nevertheless had to continue to pay full taxes to their rulers. (Moreover, in many cases these taxes were raised.) In addition they had now to supply the Russian forces with food, firewood, pack-horses and two-wheeled carts (*'araba*s) on demand and for negligible prices at best. The owners were not compensated if their horses died or their carts were broken. Furthermore, *corvée* was imposed on them, mainly for the paving and maintenance of roads. "All the economic burdens", wrote a Russian general in 1841, "of maintaining and spreading our conquests in Daghestan, lie on the small, pacified part, which has, in addition, to supply [us with] militiamen".[10]

In the political sphere, what all the rulers – even when they were initially well disposed towards Russia – were quick to find out was that Russian sovereignty was much more restrictive than the traditional patterns of dominance in the region. Rulers who openly opposed the Russians were ousted, but even those who agreed to Russian terms lost most of their power and their territories were eventually annexed.[11] Under these circumstances an atmosphere of *après moi le déluge* prevailed. The different rulers, whether out of weakness of character, despair or for other reasons, became engrossed in drinking, gambling and in some cases, debauchery. To finance these activities and/or to fill their pockets before being ousted by the Russians, they squeezed their subjects. And since their authority had already been undermined they had to use brutal force.[12]

To their subjects these rulers appeared increasingly unjust and illegitimate. The mere fact that they were appointed by the Russians in total disregard of local customs and traditions deprived them of any legitimacy. Furthermore, their behaviour, being contrary both to the *'ada* and the *shari'a*, was sheer *zulm*. This was emphasized by the increased economic burden, the responsibility for which was, to a great extent, attributed to the local rulers, and by their use of brutal force.

The contact with Russia created other changes as well, which undermined local traditions and the fabric of society. One of the most important was the introduction – planned or accidental – of alcoholic drinks on a massive scale. The results were immediate. Among the people of Aqusha, for example, who in 1819 had been praised by a Russian general "for their morality, good nature and industry [. . .] dissoluteness has already made its appearance in the wake of strong drink for which of course they had to thank Russian 'civilization'".[13] To this must be added the anti-Islamic policy of the Russians. The measures restricting Muslim religious practice, most important among which (and the cause of the greatest uproar) was the prohibition to perform the *hajj*, were reinforced by repeated though inconsistent efforts to spread (Orthodox) Christianity among the mountain people.[14] All these threatened them with loss of their identity, of their soul.

Thus, by the 1810s the people's physical and spiritual world was crumbling while they felt helpless and leaderless, and thus unable to do anything about it. At that very moment the Khalidiyya arrived on the scene with what seemed to be the right answers. The Khalidiyya spread to Daghestan via Shaykh Khalid's special deputy, Shaykh Isma'il al-Kurdumiri al-Shirwani,[15] and his disciple Shaykh Khas Muhammad al-Shirwani. The latter ordained al-Shaykh Muhammad al-Yaraghi, who in turn ordained al-Shaykh al-Sayyid Jamal al-Din al-Ghazi Ghumuqi.[16]

Like all other followers of the Naqshbandiyya-Mujaddidiyya, Shaykh Khalid believed that the *umma* had gone astray because its rulers had failed to rule according to the *shari'a* and to enforce it in public life. It was, therefore, the Shaykh's duty to guide the rulers back to the right path – that is to adherence to the *Sunna* of the Prophet and to the unequivocal fulfillment of the commandments of the *shari'a*. Otherwise, there was an implicit threat: the duty of the people to obey their rulers was valid only for as long as their orders did not contradict the *shari'a*.[17]

Accordingly, the prime concern of the first Khalidi Shaykh in Daghestan was to establish and enforce the *shari'a* and to eradicate the *'ada* in Daghestan. "Oh people", Shaykh Muhammad al-Yaraghi rebuked his listeners,

> you are neither Muslims, Christians, nor Pagans [...] The Prophet said: 'He is a true Muslim [. . .] who obeys the Qur'an and spreads my shari'a. He who acts according to my commandments will stand in Heaven higher than all the prophets who preceded Muhammad' [. . .] Pledge, oh people, to stop all your vices and henceforth to stay away from sin. Spend [your] days and nights in the mosque. Pray to God with zeal. Shed tears and ask Him to forgive you.[18]

Only following the re-establishment of the *shari'a* and the return of the Muslims to the right path, affirmed Shaykh Muhammad al-Yaraghi and Shaykh Jamal al-Din al-Ghazi Ghumuqi, would they become virtuous and strong again and would they be able "to take up arms against the unbelievers".[19] The concept of *jihad* against the invading Russians was, thus, not absent from the thought and word of the Khalidiyya in Daghestan. After all, the *shari'a* makes it obligatory on all Muslim residents of parts of *Dar al-Islam* under attack to conduct *jihad* in its defence. In propagating such views, the Khalidiyya, not surprisingly, had spectacular success in both Daghestan and Chechnya.

Still, *jihad* was clearly relegated to a second place – both in importance and in chronology.[20] Until "the right time [for *jihad*] arrived", stated both Shaykhs and their disciples, the Muslims were "allowed to submit to the Russians" and even to "give them hostages".[21] Only in 1829, when it became crystal clear that Russia was intent on the immediate and final subjugation of Daghestan and that the community remained leaderless in face of that threat, did some Khalidi activists make an extraordinary move and proclaim an *imam* to lead the *jihad*. This act, which was far from acceptable to the entire Khalidi leadership in Daghestan and therefore had to be approved again in 1830, opened a new stage in the history of Daghestan and the northern Caucasus – the thirty-year-long resistance led by the *imam*s Ghazi Muhammad (1829–32), Hamza Bek (1832–34), and the most famous and successful of them, Shamil (Shamuyil; 1834–59).[22]

While the Khalidiyya raised the banner of resistance to Russia, and led it for thirty years, the Qadiriyya arrived in the late 1850s following the defeat of resistance, in a society debilitated and dispirited by thirty years of fighting, deprivation and starvation. To begin with, three decades of intensive fighting had taken their toll in casualties. While no one has so far tried to estimate the casualties in Daghestan, present day Chechen authors have been calculating Chechen demographic losses, both direct and indirect (that is, the loss of population growth due to the fact that young men – and sometimes women as well – were killed before being able to establish a family). According to one historian the demographic damage inflicted on the Chechens between 1830 and 1860 exceeded 500,000(!).[23]

All parts of Shamil's domains suffered extreme privations, shortages and losses, but Chechnya suffered far more. The reason for this lay in the fact that from 1846 onward the Russians decided to concentrate their efforts on Chechnya, *inter alia* because it was the "bread basket" and the "soft underbelly" of Daghestan. The Russians replaced "the system of the bayonet" with "the system of the axe",[24] that is, they adopted (or rather re-adopted) a strategy of siege and attrition.[25] The intention was to "force the Chechens [...] to migrate into our territory, where no-one would disturb them any more",[26] by erecting new lines of fortifications and by conducting large-scale clearing operations of the primeval forests of Chechnya. As a rule, these clearing operations were accompanied by the systematic destruction of hamlets, supplies and gardens, by the stampeding and burning of fields and by the "confiscation" of livestock. According to a Chechen source,

> [...] Shaytan divided [the people] into several groups. Some were killed, some were exiled and some sent to far away places. The mosques of the men and the praying places of the women were turned into pig-sties [...][27]

The Chechens had thus either to submit or to migrate into the mountains and live there on the verge of starvation. According to the Imam and the Khalidi masters, submission to the Russians meant reneging on Islam and losing salvation in the afterlife. Nevertheless, the Chechens had increasingly been forced by sheer starvation to turn to the Russians. By March 1853 the situation had grown so difficult that Shamil asked the Ottoman Sultan for help. "We have lost our strength", he wrote, and "have no force to furnish against our enemies. We are deprived of means and are now in a disastrous position."[28] After the Crimean War the situation vis-à-vis the final assault by the Russians had become desperate. In 1858 Shamil asked to be informed

> if the Sublime Porte has any expectations of a war with Russia, to create a diversion in his favour within a reasonable period of time, say a few years, in which case he will still hold on in the hope of giving and receiving support, but that otherwise he will be forced to put an end to the bloody war.[29]

Once again, the people were helpless and leaderless while their physical and spiritual world was crumbling. And once again a Sufi brotherhood arrived on the scene at the right moment with the right answers.

The man who introduced the Qadiriyya into the Caucasus was al-Shaykh al-Hajj Kunta al-Michiki al-Iliskhani.[30] A promising scholar and a disciple of the Khalidiyya, he was initiated into the Qadiriyya during a *hajj* undertaken in 1848–9. His followers believe that he was taught and initiated by 'Abd al-Qadir al-Gilani himself during a dream in the saint's mausoleum in Baghdad, which perhaps reflects the Qadiri initiation ceremony.[31] Having started to proselytize for the new *tariqa* upon his return, Shaykh Kunta was soon exiled on a second *hajj* by Imam Shamil. He returned only after the collapse of the Khalidi-led Imamate.

Being a Qadiri, Shaykh Kunta laid emphasis on individual rather than on communal salvation. Thus, he appealed to his fellow-Muslims to withdraw from worldly affairs and concentrate on prayer and on the individual endeavour to improve one's own morality. Each Muslim had, according to Shaykh Kunta, [to]

> clean his soul and interior from the dirt and everything that is forbidden and [...] from evil intentions and falsehoods. Then remember Me and call Me for help, and he will surely find Me in his soul and heart. Indeed My dwelling is the human heart and if [a servant] cleans his heart and fills it with recollection of Me [dhikr] then I will instantly enter his soul and will find him before he finds Me.[32]

Furthermore, in collective affairs – or politics – he demanded the cessation of resistance to the Russians, which he deemed not only futile but also a sin against God. He even predicted the downfall of the Khalidi-led Imamate. This did not mean, however, acceptance of Russian rule, but rather what might be termed in modern terminology "passive resistance":

> As for the teaching of the 'ulama' that the faithful should not communicate with the infidels and should separate themselves by prayer, it is true indeed.[33]

By this means Shaykh Kunta added a third, more realistic option to the two set out by the Khalidiyya – submission, which enjoyed the same rank as deserting Islam or resistance. They could now submit to Russia's superior might and still remain "good Muslims":

> God Almighty in His mercy gives those imprisoned or captured or held by the infidels recompense as if they performed the pilgrimage or recited the Qur'an and [treats them] like children who do not have to perform religious rituals, but who still perform them and [grants them] as if they had undertaken all nawa'if [...][34]

He thus offered a people approaching the limit of their ability to suffer and on the verge of falling into bottomless despair a way out of the abyss. He supplied them with the religious legitimation to end their armed struggle and gave them hope of salvation. Furthermore, Shaykh Kunta took care to make those opting for his course proud: according to him they were the best of Muslims and their faith was superior to that of the Meccans, "because here [in Mecca] you have only one enemy [Shaytan] and there we have three – Shaytan, infidels [*kafirun*] and hypocrites [*munafiqun*]". [35]

It is not surprising, therefore, that thousands flocked to the Shaykh and accepted his authority. However this soon aroused the suspicion of the Russian administration, which on 15 January 1864 arrested Hajj Kunta. The Shaykh was exiled to the town of Ustiuzhko in the province of Novgorod where according to official Russian documents he died on 31 May 1867. His followers deny his death to this very day. Hajj Kunta's arrest was followed by the incident known as *sha'ltan tom* ("the Battle of Daggers") in which demonstrators appealing for his release were shot at by the Russian army,[36] and steps were taken to uproot the Qadiriyya.[37]

Far from being uprooted, the Qadiriyya re-emerged after an initial period of confusion following its Shaykh's arrest. In the absence of its founder, however, the Qadiriyya had ceased to be a united movement and split into several branches. More dramatically, the Qadiriyya, which had started as a movement opposing armed resistance to Russia, turned into its sworn enemy. Henceforth branches of the Qadiriyya would take part in all, and lead many of, the uprisings against Russian rule – Tsarist, Soviet and post-Soviet alike.[38] By the 1890s the Qadiriyya had all but replaced the Khalidiyya among the lowland and foothill Chechens and recruited the Ingush and the Ghumuqs to the *tariqa*.[39] It had been unable, however, to establish itself in Daghestan (as well as among the mountain Chechens). There, in Daghestan, the Khalidiyya has remained firmly entrenched, though a new branch preaching acceptance of infidel rule has gradually taken over.[40] Several explanations can be offered for these facts.

One already mentioned above is that – at least in the initial stage – the Qadiriyya supplied the Chechens with a way out from a dead end at a moment when their physical, spiritual and moral worlds had collapsed under the blows of the Russian armies. Soon enough, however, Russian maladministration and persecution revived the bitter memories and resentment of the Chechens and pushed the Qadiriyya to lead resistance to infidel rule. In a self-reinforcing circle this helped to increase the Qadiriyya's appeal to the Chechens, while its growing popularity enhanced its position of leadership of the struggle. The Daghestanis had also been subjected to the deprivations of war, but not to such an extreme. They, therefore, had not become disenchanted with the Khalidiyya and it continued to lead their resistance until at least the 1920s. At this stage the fact that the Qadiriyya had become anti-Russian left to those Daghestanis (and Chechens) disillusioned with resistance under the devastating blows of the "Godless Armies" with no alternative to the quietist branch of the Khalidiyya.

Another explanation lays emphasis on the fact that Hajj Kunta introduced the Qadiri loud *dhikr* performed by chanting and dancing, as opposed to the Naqshbandi silent *dhikr*. This must have made an important difference because the Chechens were relative "newcomers" to Islam in comparison with the Daghestanis. The islamization of Daghestan had started in the seventh and had been completed by the fifteenth century. The islamization of the Chechens had begun only in the seventeenth century and had been completed as late as during the Khalidi-led Imamate in the first half of the nineteenth century. The Chechens, therefore, being less deeply islamized than the Daghestanis, less observant of the *shari'a* and more attached to pre-Islamic beliefs and practices, were in stronger need of such a ritual than their neighbours to the east.

Both explanations are only partial and they are not entirely satisfactory even if combined. The first one is very complex, contains internal contradictions and explains individual episodes and phases rather than the entire process. The second explanation is again partial since the Khalidiyya had also practised loud *dhikr* ceremonies before the advent of the Qadiriyya.[41] Thus, we need to seek other explanations which can combine with these to clarify the situation in a more comprehensive way.

One further explanation also has to do with the difference in the degree of islamization. Not only had Daghestan been islamized earlier and therefore also more deeply than Chechnya, but since the eleventh century it had been a major centre of Islamic learning, to such a degree that, at least until the beginning of the twentieth century, it supplied spiritual leadership to the entire northern Caucasus. Accordingly, the *'ulama'* had come to enjoy a leading role in the spiritual and secular lives of the Daghestanis. The Naqshbandiyya with its traditional emphasis on learning had throughout its history a great appeal to *'ulama'*. Naturally, the Khalidiyya held the same attraction to the *'ulama'* in Daghestan and the people followed them on this matter as on many others.

The Naqshbandiyya's insistence on learning the *shari'a*, not only adhering to it, had traditionally made it an exclusive *tariqa*. Even the Khalidiyya, which had deliberately made an effort to reach the entire community and the lower strata of society, remained fairly exclusive. The Qadiriyya traditionally had a different stand. While demanding adherence to the *shari'a*, it also emphasized the importance of the Shaykh and full obedience to him. It made a distinction between *shari'a* and *tariqa* and did not oblige its Shaykhs to be *'ulama'* as well. "What the *'ulama'* say" about learning, stated Shaykh Hajj Kunta,

> is true for an ustadh of the shari'a [an 'alim] but not the ustadh of a tariqa [a Sufi Shaykh], who does not have to go deep into studying madhhabs. [The aim of the ustadh of the tariqa] is to place himself between God and His servants and act as their mediator. It is a great assignment. And this assignment will not be fulfilled through learning 'ulum and studying madhhabs but only through reaching God and through looking into Him with seeing eyes and by loving God and His Prophet and by following divine laws strictly.[42]

Naturally such a stand seems to have suited the Chechens more.

But this explanation too fails to provide a satisfactory answer even in combination with the first two. A fourth explanation seems to be needed to complete the picture. This has to do with the fact that all the Shaykhs of the Qadiriyya have been Vainakh (Chechen and Ingush). The Chechens had been accustomed to following the leadership of Daghestan in matters pertaining to Islam and to getting most if not all of their religious leaders from there. And even though there had in the past been Chechen *'ulama'* and Khalidi Shaykhs, they had all been educated in Daghestan and had a foreign flavour to them. Shaykh Kunta and his disciples and successors have all been Chechens "uncontaminated" by external education. They have, thus, been able to speak – both metaphorically and literally – to the people in their own language.

This fact must have facilitated the spread of the Qadiriyya among the Vainakh. At the same time this same fact must have been a determinant in arresting the spread of this *tariqa* in Daghestan. The Daghestanis – and the Avars in particular – have been accustomed to holding leadership positions vis-à-vis the Chechens and have traditionally looked down on them (and indeed still do). It was, therefore, inconceivable for them to accept Chechen leadership, not to say the authority of a Chechen religious master.

No doubt, other reasons must have existed for the rapid spread of the Qadiriyya among the Chechens and its relative failure in Daghestan. Nevertheless, the combination of the four reasons counted above supplies one with a fairly satisfactory explanation for that phenomenon.

NOTES

1   See chapter by Shikhsaidov in this volume.

2   The first to use the term *ta'ifa* in Western scholarship was J. Spencer Trimingham, *Sufi Orders in Islam* (Oxford, 1971). Nehemia Levtzion and John O. Voll have borrowed his terminology (though not his chronology); see their "Introduction" to Nehemia Levtzion and John O. Voll (eds.), *Eighteenth Century Revival in Islam* (Syracuse, 1982), pp. 3-20. For the term "neo-Sufism" see, for example, Octave Depont, *Les confréries religieuses musulmanes* (Paris, 1987).

3   The best description of the *Sufi ta'ifas* in the Northern Caucasus (although it deals mainly with the Qadiriyya) is Chantal Lemercier-Quelquejay, 'Les tariqat au Caucase du Nord', in A. Popovic and C. Veinstein (eds.), *Les ordres mystiques dans l'Islam: Cheminements et situation actuelle* (Paris, 1986), pp. 7-38. See also Alexandre Bennigsen and Chantal Lemercier-Quelquejay, *Le Soufi et le commissaire. Les confréries musulmanes en URSS* (Paris, 1986); Alexandre Bennigsen and S. Enders Wimbush, *Muslims of the Soviet Empire. A Guide* (London, 1985). And see notes 27, 38 below.

4   According to local tradition, the first Naqshbandi-Mujaddidi leader in the Caucasus was Shaykh Mansur, who was in many respects the precursor of the movement in the nineteenth century. However, he did not establish the order in the Caucasus. The most recent work on Shaykh Mansur is Sharpuddin Ahmadov, *Imam Mansur (narodno-osvoboditel'noe dvizhenie v Chechne i na Severnom Kavkaze v kontse XVIIIv.)* (Groznyi, 1991). Still of great value is Alexandre Bennigsen, 'Un mouvement populaire au Caucase du XVIIIe siècle: La "guerre sainte" du Sheikh Mansur (1785-1794). Page mal connue et controversée des relations Russo-Turques', *Cahiers du monde Russe et Soviétique*, Vol. V, No. 2 (April-June 1964), pp. 159-205.

5   The best overviews of the Naqshbandiyya and its history are still Hamid Algar's 'A Brief History of the Naqshbandi Order', in Marc Gaborieau, Alexandre Popovic and Thierry Zarcone (eds.), *Naqshbandis. Historical Developments and Present Situation of a Muslim Mystical Order* (Istanbul, 1990), pp. 3-44 (which partly replaces his 'The Naqshbandi Order: A Preliminary Survey of its History and Significance', *Studia Islamica*, 44 (1970), pp. 123-52) and his 'The Present State of Naqshbandi Studies', in Gaborieau, Popovic and Zarcone (eds.), *op.cit.*, pp. 45-56.

6   Trimingham, *op. cit.*, p. 63.

7   Bernard Lewis, *The Middle East and the West* (New York, 1966, p/b), p. 97. The most comprehensive study of Sirhindi is Yohanan Friedman, *Shaykh Ahmad Sirhindi: An Outline of His Thought and a Study of His Image in the Eyes of Posterity* (Montreal, 1971).

8   For Shaykh Khalid, see Butrus Abu-Manneh, 'The Naqshbandiyya-Mujaddidiyya in the Ottoman Lands in the Early 19th Century', *Die Welt des Islams*, XXII (1982), pp. 1-12 (hereafter: Abu-Manneh); Albert Hourani, 'Sufism and Modern Islam: Maulana Khalid and the Naqshbandi Order', in *id., The Emergence of the Middle East* (London, 1981), pp. 75-89.

9   The best overview of the Qadiriyya is still Trimingham, *op. cit.*

10   *Dvizhenie*, pp. 312-24, document No. 168, 'Excerpt from Survey of the Disastrous Situation in Northern Daghestan, with a Short Outline of Preceding Events' [by Klüge-von-Klugenau], 31 December 1841 [12 January 1842], p. 323.

11   Muriel Atkin, *Russia and Iran, 1780-1828* (Minneapolis, 1980), p. 165.

12   One such ruler, much trusted and respected by the Russians, was Aghalar Bek, the *de facto* ruler of Ghazi-Ghumuq in the 1840s and 1850s. He was described as spending his time in endless drinking sessions. Any servant who was not quick enough to serve him a bottle would be pricked by a fork, a knife or any other instrument that happened to be in the Bek's hand. By "indiscriminate beating and flogging" he "severely inculcated reverence towards the Russians in his people [. . .] The entire Khanate trembled before him." But, states the Russian source, "the people had become used" to his behaviour "and though afraid of the *khan*, they were devoted to him"; Viacheslav Soltan, 'Obzor sobytii v Dagestane v 1855 i 1856 godakh', *Kavkazskii sbornik*, XII, pp. 503-05. This last sentence obviously testifies more to Russian psychology than to the situation in that Khanate.

13   John F. Baddeley, *The Russian Conquest of the Caucasus* (London, 1908), p. 134.

14   A Russian document stated with rare and unusual candour: "A complete rapprochement between them and us can be expected only when the Cross is set up on the mountains and in the valleys and when temples for Christ the Saviour replace the mosques. Until then the force of arms is the sole true bastion of our rule in the Caucasus"; M.O. Kosven and Kh.-M.O. Khashaev (eds.), *Istoriia, geografiia i etnografiia Dagestana XVIII–XIX vv. Arkhivnye materialy* (Moscow, 1958), pp. 362-68 ('Historical Survey of the Samur District' by André de Simon, 1819. Quotation from p. 367).

15   See chapter by Abu-Manneh in this volume.

16   Al-Shaykh al-Sayyid Jamal al-Din al-Ghazi Ghumuqi al-Daghistani, *Al-Adab al-Mardiyya fi al-Tariqa al-Naqshbandiyya* (Petrovsk, 1905), p. 80. For the spread of the Khalidiyya, see Moshe Gammer, 'The Beginnings of the Naqshbandiyya in Daghestan and the Russian Conquest of the Caucasus', *Die Welt des Islams*, 34 (1994), pp. 204-17; Michael Kemper, 'Einige Notizien zur Arabischsprachigen Literatur

der *ihad*-Bewegung in Dagestan und Tschetschenien in der ersten Hälfte des 19. Jarhunderts', in Anke von Kügelgen, Michael Kemper and Allen J. Frank (eds.), *Muslim Culture in Russia and Central Asia from the 18th to the Early 20th Century*, 2: *Inter-Regional and Inter-Ethnic Relations* (Berlin, 1998), pp. 63-99; Clemens P. Sidorko, 'Die Naqšbandiyya im nordöstlichen Kaukazus: Ein Historischer Überblick', *Asiatische Studien*, LI, No. 2 (1997), pp. 627-50; Anna Zelkina, *In Quest for God and Freedom. Sufi Responses to the Russian Advance in the North Caucasus* (London, 2000), pp. 100-15.

17   Shaykh Khalid's disciples in the Caucasus developed this notion even further: Muhammad al-Yaraghi is reported to have stated that "a Muslim should be no one's slave [but God's] and should not pay any taxes, not even to a Muslim [ruler]. A Muslim must be a free man and equality must reign among the believers", A.A. Neverovskii, *O Nachale bezpokoistv v Severnom i Srednem Dagestane* (St. Petersburg, 1847), p. 5.

18   Muhammad al-Yaraghi as quoted ibid., pp. 5-6. A somewhat different and shorter version was published in *Voina*, X, p. 20. Yet another, longer version was printed in Kuzanov, 'Miuridizm v Dagestane', *Raduga*, 1861, No. 2, pp. 32-3.

19   Neverovskii, *op. cit.*, p. 6.

20   I differ on this point both from Russian/Soviet historiography and from Zelkina (*op. cit.*, pp. 116-19), who, though for completely different reasons, exaggerate the importance of *jihad* in the preaching of al-Yaraghi in the early and mid-1820s.

21   Muhammad al-Yaraghi to the Community of Chirkah, as published in *Voina*, X, p. 28. Neverovskii, *op. cit.* (pp. 13-14) attributes this speech to Ghazi Muhammad.

22   Moshe Gammer, *Muslim Resistance to the Tsar: Shamil and the Conquest of Chechnia and Daghestan* (London, 1994); Zelkina, *op. cit.*

23   Mayrbek Vachagaeyev, 'Chechnia v Kavkazskoi voine, 1816–1859' (Moscow, 1995; unpublished dissertation), p. 35.

24   Arnold Zisserman, 'Otryvki iz moikh vospominanii', *Russkii vestnik*, 1876, No. 4, p. 424.

25   Moshe Gammer, 'Russian Strategies in the Conquest of Chechnia and Daghestan', in Marie Bennigsen Broxup (ed.), *The North Caucasus Barrier: The Russian Advance towards the Muslim World* (London, 1992), pp. 45-61.

26   "K.", 'Levyi flang Kavkazskoi linii v 1848 godu', *Kavkazskii sbornik*, Vol. XI, p. 349.

27   'Abd al-Salam, as quoted in Anna Zelkina, 'Some aspects of the Teaching of Kunta Hajji on the Basis of a Manuscript by 'Abd al-Salam Written in 1862 AD', *Journal of the History of Sufism*, 1-2 (2000), p. 486.

28   *Shamil – stavlennik sultanskoi Turtsii i angliiskikh kolonizatorov* (Tbilisi, 1953), p. 367, document No. 302, Shamil's letter to the Sultan, 1853 [not later than 7 April]. Even if the terms of this letter are exaggerated (as might be expected in a request for help), it still shows the situation and state of mind of its sender and his people.

29   UK, Public Record Office, Foreign Office Archives, FO/78/1435, O'Brian to Bulwer, Private, Constantinople, 4 August (copy), appended to Bulwer to Rassel, No. 151, Therapia, 13 September 1859.

30   The latest and best study so far of Kunta Hajji is Vahit Akayev, *Sheikh Kunta Khadzhi: Zhizn' i uchenie* (Groznyi, 1994).

31   "In the initiation ceremony recorded by J.P. Brown, *loc. cit.* [John Porter Brown, *The Darvishes: or, Oriental Spiritualism* (London, 1868)], the candidate for admission to the Order sees 'Abd al-Ḳadir in dreams" – D.S. Margoliouth, "Ḳadiriyya", *EI*, Vol. IV, p. 381.

32   'Abd al-Salam, as quoted in Zelkina, *op. cit.*, p. 491.

33   Ibid., p. 492.

34   Ibid., p. 494.

35   Ibid., *loc. cit.*

36   As soon as the adherents of the Shaykh heard of his arrest they started to flock to Shali, believing that Hajj Kunta was being held in the Russian fort nearby. Three delegations approached the commander of the fort, but their request for his release met with a flat refusal. By 26 January 1864 about 3000 men and women had gathered in Shali. After the third delegation was rejected they started a continuous *dhikr*. On 30 January the crowd, having completed their morning ablution and prayer, threw away their firearms and moved towards the fort. The Russian troops forming a *carrée* in front of the citadel fired in volleys at the approaching men and women. The Chechens then stormed the troops with their daggers and were met by grapeshot. Russian sources give different figures of Chechens killed that day, ranging from 100 to "more than 400" of whom four to six were women. The Russian losses were reported as 8 killed and 33 wounded.

37   These included massive arrests, the prohibition of *dhikr* and efforts to prompt the followers of the Qadiriyya to emigrate to the Ottoman Empire.

38   For the further history of the Qadiriyya, see Alexandre Bennigsen, 'The Qadiriyyah (Kunta Hajji) *Tariqah* in North-East Caucasus: 1850–1987', *Islamic Culture*, LXII, Nos. 2-3 (April-July 1988); Moshe Gammer, 'The Qadiriyya in the Northern Caucasus', *Journal of the History of Sufism*, Volume 1-2 (October 2000; Special Issue: *The Qadiriyya Sufi Order*), pp. 275–94.

39   Its hostility to Russian rule might, in fact, have facilitated the Qadiriyya's spread among the Chechens and Ingush, adding on the other hand its share to their ongoing insubordination.

40   See chapter by Michael Kemper in this volume.

41   E.g., Nikolai A. Volkonskii, 'Sem' Let v Plenu na Kavkaze (1849–1856). Ocherk Politicheskogo i Domashnego Byta Kavkazskikh Gortsev', *Voennyi Vestnik*, 1882, No. 5, p. 278.

42   'Abd al-Salam, as quoted in Zelkina, *op. cit.*, p. 487.

THE ROLE OF SHAYKH ISMA'IL AL-SHIRWANI IN THE KHALIDI SUB-ORDER

BUTRUS ABU-MANNEH

THE MAKING OF A SUFI SHAYKH

At the beginning of the 19th century, following the decline of Persian (Qajar) rule over Daghestan, the Russians invaded the country and captured Derbend (1806). In the peace treaty of Gulistan (1813) between them, Persia renounced its claim over the country.[1] When certain local princes formed an alliance against Russian domination they were crushed and between 1818 and 1820 the greater part of the country fell under direct Russian rule.[2]

While these events were taking place, Daghestan was witnessing a revival of Sunni Islamic learning. From a recently published collection of biographies of Daghestani 'ulama' of the late 12th and 13th centuries/late 18th and 19th centuries,[3] we learn of a growing eagerness among a younger generation for learning Islamic subjects and for running life according to the tenets of the shari'a. We learn moreover of leading scholars such as Sa'id al-Harakani and Muhammad al-Yaraghi, both of whom were highly regarded in Daghestan and attracted many students.[4] Other students went to study with teachers in Anatolian towns. One of these was Isma'il al-Kurdemiri, the subject of this paper. Indeed while the Russians depended in their government on the old social classes and upon customary law, a new generation was being introduced to Sunni-Islamic concepts and to the role that the shari'a should play in Muslim society.

However, Sunni-Islamic learning alone was not what motivated the people of these regions throughout the 19th century. Their convictions were invigorated by the expansion, at about the same time, of a Sufi orthodox order, the Naqshbandiyya-Khalidiyya, which was carried into Daghestan by shaykh Isma'il al-Kurdemiri and met with instant success there.

Isma'il was born in 1197/1783 in the village of Kurd Emir in the sub-district of Shamakhi (in Russian Shemakha) to the west of Baku in the Khanate of Shirvan and is known as

Kurdemiri, after his birth place. But following his departure from Shirvan and his immigration to Anatolia, he came to be called Shirwani. As a boy, Isma'il started studying with Muhammad Nuri of Shamakhi.[5] In 1800 he moved to Erzinjan in the northeastern region of Anatolia to study with shaykh Evliya-zade Abdulrahman. His second location in Anatolia was Tokat where he spent several years before moving to Baghdad to study *hadith* with the well-known Kurdish *'alim* shaykh Yahya al-Mazzuri of the town of 'Amadiyya in Iraqi Kurdistan. He also studied there what was called *ulum hikamiyye* (sciences), with Mulla Muhammad ibn Adam. His next location was Burdur (Bouldour) in the south-western region of Anatolia (in 1220/1805) where he studied certain legal manuals.[6] A year later, he returned to Shirvan and took up the teaching of Islamic subjects, continuing in this activity for the next seven years

In the *hajj* season of 1227/1812 he went on pilgrimage to Mecca.[7] On his way back he visited Medina and Jerusalem and continued onward to Istanbul where he stayed for several months (1228/1813). We do not know the object of his visit to this city, but like many young men of deep religious convictions at that time, and judging from his next move, Isma'il al-Kurdemiri was presumably looking for a Sufi guide (*murshid*). In Istanbul it is possible that he was advised to seek initiation into the Naqshbandi-Mujaddidi order at the hands of shaykh Abdullah al-Dihlawi (known also as Shah Ghulam 'Ali) in Delhi, who was perhaps the leading shaykh of this order at the time.[8] But at Basra he seems to have heard about shaykh Khalid, who was known as a *khalifa* (deputy) of shaykh Abdullah and who had returned just two years earlier from Delhi. This led Isma'il to decide to seek initiation into the order at the hands of shaykh Khalid.[9] As a result, he left Basra and came to Baghdad where the shaykh was staying for a short while (1228/1813) and became his disciple, and when Khalid returned to Sulaymaniyya afterwards, he accompanied him and stayed with him there.

Isma'il al-Kurdemiri was one of the first disciples of shaykh Khalid. Perhaps because of that, the shaykh invested much time and effort in training him in the rites and teachings of the Naqshbandi-Mujaddidi order. In addition, following the tradition that Naqshbandi shaykhs should be learned in the sciences of Islam, Isma'il was made to carry out further studies in these subjects (*'ulum-i zahire ve batine*).[10]

According to a *levha* (tablet) written in Arabic and hung on the wall of the mausoleum of Shirwani in Amasya which Mahmud Kemal Inal (d.1957), the Ottoman historian and biographer, copied and which gives what can be termed the official biography of the shaykh,[11] Ismaʿil stayed at the *zawiya*s of shaykh Khalid, in Baghdad and in Sulaymaniyya, until 1233/1817–18. This period of about four years is an exceptionally long period in the Khalidi tradition.[12] It suggests that Ismaʿil al-Kurdemiri acquired his training by way of *suhba*, according to which a *murid* associates with a "perfect shaykh", stays at his *zawiya* for a long period, sometimes for years, throughout which he frequently attends his presence, serves him and submits to his instruction. Only when the shaykh is convinced that he has been trained well enough in the rites of the order, is well acquainted with its teachings and is ready to carry on its message does he ordain him as his deputy (*khalifa*) and send him to spread the order to a place assigned for him by the shaykh.[13]

In this sense and as an early disciple of shaykh Khalid, Ismaʿil was privileged to be trained in this way because Khalid, having been ambitious to spread the order far and wide, found the way of *suhba* slow and calling for time and expense, both of which he lacked. Consequently he introduced the rite of khalwa arbaʿiniyya, or forty days retreat, to provide intensive training for his disciples and deputies, a practice regarded as an innovation in the Naqshbandi-Mujaddidi order.[14]

At any rate, in that year (i.e., in 1233) shaykh Ismaʿil was ordained as a *khalifa* (deputy) of shaykh Khalid. He was not an ordinary deputy but one upon whom was bestowed *khilafa mutlaqa*, or absolute successorship, and he was ordered to return to Shirvan and spread the order in these regions.[15] It is claimed that on this occasion Khalid gave him the title of Siraj al-Din (the light of religion)[16] as he did to his other early *khalifa*, ʿUthman Tawila.[17]

THE EXPANSION OF THE KHALIDIYYA IN DAGHESTAN

Shaykh Ismaʿil was not the first shaykh to carry the Naqshbandi order into the Caucasus. This title is claimed for shaykh Mansur Ushurma, a Chechen, who introduced the order into the northern Caucasus.[18] According to a Russian claim, Mansur was initiated in Bukhara but according to Hasan al-Alqadari of Daghestan, he was initiated in the Ottoman Empire, which appears more likely.[19] Shaykh Mansur fought the Russians from the mid-1780s and "tried to arouse the western Caucasian Circassian tribes" against them but he was captured in 1791 and died in prison two years later.[20]

However, the movement of Imam Mansur (as he is sometimes called) did not strike roots in the Caucasus; "the Naqshbandiyya vanished from the Caucasian scene for the next thirty years" in the words of Bennigsen and Wimbush.[21] It was left indeed to the militant Khalidiyya to penetrate the region through the efforts of shaykh Isma'il who took up his mission in his native region, Shirvan, about a generation after the capture of shaykh Mansur.

In the meantime, Shirvan fell under Russian domination. First, in 1805, Mustafa, the Khan of Shirvan, submitted to Russian suzerainty.[22] But in the summer of 1820, following prolonged Russian pressure on him, Mustafa escaped to Persia, after which his territory was finally annexed to the Russian dominions and proclaimed a Russian province.[23] Thus about three years after his return from Iraq, shaykh Isma'il found his country falling under direct Russian rule.

The subjugation of the region to Russian rule revealed the weakness and incoherence of those Muslim communities of the north and north-east Caucasus. Customary law prevailed at the expense of the *shar'i* law, tribal habits of blood revenge were the norm, and alcohol drinking was "on a massive scale".[24] In short there existed a moral and religious laxity which made these communities extremely vulnerable and unprepared to face foreign, not to say Christian, domination. The answer for such a situation was the return to Islam and to orthodox Islamic ideals and values. (In his despair, shaykh Sa'id al-Harakani advised emigration to the Muslim holy cities.)[25]

The Khalidiyya which shaykh Isma'il carried to Shirvan and Daghestan emphasized, like its mother order, the Naqshbandiyya-Mujaddidiyya, the duty of the Muslim believer to follow strictly the precepts of the *shari'a* and to guide his life according to the *sunna* of the Prophet. The way of the Naqshbandis wrote Sirhindi, "is absolutely identical with that of the Companions (of the Prophet)".[26] This dictum, frequently repeated in Naqshbandi literature, is central to Khalidi teaching. Khalid seems to have been of the belief that the Muslim *umma* had gone astray. Thus, in order to restore it to the right path, the period of the Prophet and his Companions should be brought to the forefront as an ideal to be recaptured by Muslims.[27] In other words the expansion of the Naqshbandi-Mujaddidi order and its branch, the Khalidiyya, carried with it a revivalist message of Islam. Indeed, wherever Khalid's emissaries reached, Islamic zeal was aroused and adherents of the *shari'a* multiplied.

Shaykh Isma'il preached the Khalidiyya in Shirvan and Daghestan for over eight years. During this time he trained and initiated many disciples, mostly from the Caucasus but also from Qazan and other Muslim regions in Russia. "Isma'il ... made Shirvan ... a centre of Tarikat teaching of the ... Nakshibandi" order, writes Baddeley.[28] A recently published biography names several deputies whom he ordained in Daghestan.[29] One of the most famous of these was perhaps Khas Muhammad of Shirvan who as a young man studied with shaykh Muhammad al-Yaraghi, who was a highly regarded scholar in Daghestan at the time. After becoming a *khalifa* of shaykh Isma'il, he went back to his former teacher and initiated him into the Khalidi sub-order. He then accompanied him on a long visit to shaykh Isma'il, after which Yaraghi was ordained by the shaykh as a *khalifa* in the Khalidi suborder.[30] In the light of the role played by Khas Muhammad and Yaraghi after that, especially the contribution of the latter to the founding of the *murid* movement, it is perhaps not too far from the truth to suggest that the mission of shaykh Isma'il laid the foundations for a religious and socio-political revival among the North Caucasian Muslim communities in the second quarter of the nineteenth century.[31]

In other words, the expansion of the Khalidiyya into Shirvan and Daghestan was not the same as the spread of any other order but carried with it a strong message of a return to a way of life in accordance with the *ahl al-sunna* and following the tenets of the *shari'a*. In short, Khalidi teachings were strict in their call to abide by *shari'a* rules and militant in their attitude towards moral laxity and disbelief.[32]

After the annexation of Shirvan by the Russians, shaykh Isma'il, called by now Mawlana (our master),[33] indicating the respect in which his disciples held him, became the centre of a circle of followers dedicated to the cause of the Khalidiyya. When disturbances took place in Daghestan and Ghabarta in 1825-26, which were attributed to the preaching of Muhammad al-Yaraghi,[34] the Russian authorities had a better appraisal of this religious movement. Accordingly they exiled two of the shaykh's deputies into interior Russia but he himself was saved from a similar fate due to his popularity in Shirvan, and, more likely perhaps, also due to the intervention of the ex-Khan's wife Fatma (Gulandam Hanım).[35] But a little later (1242/1826–7) he "was forced to emigrate to Turkey" i.e., Anatolia, and never returned to the Caucasus.[36] His legacy remained as part of the modern social and religious history of Daghestan, but this is beyond the theme of this paper especially as several books and articles have lately been published on this subject.[37]

It seems to have been the policy of the Russians that whenever they conquered a Muslim region and were faced with unrest, they put pressure upon members of the Muslim elite to migrate. Thus when they occupied the Crimea and a little later annexed it (1783) many members of the Tatar upper classes migrated to the Ottoman lands where they were settled in towns in Anatolia. The same policy was applied when Russia annexed the Caucasian Muslim regions in the course of the 19th century. Consequently, we find that from about the end of the 18th century immigrant communities from the Crimea, from Daghestan, and Shirvan, and later from Chechnya and Circassia settled in the Anatolian towns and the countryside. By 1864 according to more than one estimate several hundred thousand had migrated into Anatolia alone.[38]

After his expulsion from Shirvan, shaykh Isma'il first settled in Ahiska on the eastern Anatolian Black Sea coast. But when the Russians occupied that place in the war of 1828–29,[39] he settled in Amasya in the north-central region of Anatolia and stayed there for four years. According to Xalilli, many of his disciples seem to have joined him there.[40] After that he moved to Sivas, south-east of Amasya, and remained there for nine years spreading Khalidi teachings. In 1841 he returned to Amasya permanently and died there in August 1848.[41] Whether he maintained connections with his followers in the Caucasus during this period is an open question.

We do not know how shaykh Isma'il lived in Anatolia. On the whole the Ottoman sultans extended support to Sufi shaykhs. But throughout the 1830s the state was busy with the conflict with Muhammad 'Ali and it is doubtful whether a newly arrived shaykh could find such help. However, as soon as this conflict appeared to be approaching an end, and following the rise of Sultan Abdülmecid, shaykh Isma'il seems to have used the opportunity to apply for an allowance from the state and in March 1840 he was granted a monthly allowance of 200 kurush "from the poll tax (*jizya*) income" apparently of the province of Sivas.[42] In the same *irade* four other Sufi shaykhs of Eastern Anatolia were given allowances as well.[43]

Throughout his career of over thirty years as a Khalidi shaykh, Isma'il kept his allegiance to shaykh Khalid and his teachings, with a single exception, while he was still in Shirvan. Having met with much success in his mission in the north Caucasian regions and having ordained a number of prominent deputies (*khalifa*s), he probably felt he deserved a place among the great shaykhs of the order. Thus, he started asking his followers to link with his image (i.e., to practice the *rabit a* with the Naqshbandi *silsila*, or chain, of the masters of the order) with his image first, before that of shaykh Khalid, contrary to the instructions of the latter. The implication of this move in the Sufi tradition was an expression of a desire to separate from the mother order (i.e., the Khalidiyya) and to establish a sub-order of his own. When the matter became known to shaykh Khalid he wrote to Isma'il threatening him with expulsion from the order if he continued to pursue that course (this was similar to what he had done for instance with his deputy in Istanbul Abdulwahhab al-Susi). Following the warnings shaykh Isma'il retreated and retained his allegiance to his master until the end of his life, even after the death of shaykh Khalid (see Khalid's letter in the appendix).[44]

Shaykh Isma'il lived a little over twenty years in Anatolia and died in Amasya in Ramadan 1264/August 1848. Over his tomb, his son Mehmed Rushdi built a mausoleum and a mosque (1869–70).[45] His tomb became a place of pilgrimage for many of his followers.

Shaykh Isma'il had four sons. The first, Abdulhamid, was born in Shirvan but died in 1846 in Amasya, during the lifetime of his father. The second, Mehmed Rushdi, known in Ottoman history by the family name of Shirvani-zade, was born in Amasya (in 1245/1829-30) about two years after the immigration of his father. He studied religious sciences and at the age of twenty-two he continued his studies in Istanbul where he became a student of the famous *'alim* Vidinli Mustafa Efendi. Protected by the ªeyhül-Islam Arif Hikmet Bey, who was of strong Naqshbandi-Mujaddidi tendencies, Mehmed Rushdi first entered the Ilmiye and became an instructor at the medresse of Bayezid. But early in the 1860s, on the advice of Fuad Pasha, he shifted to the Mulkiye (i.e., the civil service). Soon after he was sent out as Governor-General of Damascus from where he was promoted in 1865 to the rank of Minister of Endowments. In 1873, he was appointed by Sultan Abdülaziz to the post of Grand Vizier, in which he served for about ten months. He died as Vali (Governor-General) of the Hijaz a year later.[46]

Isma'il's third son, Ahmet Hulusi, was born in Sivas and also studied religious sciences and became an *'alim*. He entered the legal system and reached the high rank of *Qadi* of Istanbul (1874) and was promoted to the titular rank of *Kaziasker* of Anatolia. Moreover, he served as a member of the committee that authored the *Mecelle*. Ahmed Hulusi was one of the two leading *'ulama'* in Istanbul who aroused the *Softas* to demonstrate against the Grand

Vizier Mahmud Nedim in May 1876. This led to the downfall of the Grand Vizier and initiated the events which led to the deposition of Sultan Abdülaziz.[47] After the rise of Sultan Abdülhamid II, Ahmed Hulusi was sent on a mission to Afghanistan (1877). On his way back, before reaching Istanbul, he received a letter of nomination as *na'ib* (local *shar'i* judge) of Diyarbekir (1878). Two years later when his term of office ended he was ordered to stay at Amasya where he died nine years later.[48] Like his two elder brothers, Isma'il's fourth son, Mustafa Nuri, worked in the government service and became a high official in the treasury in Istanbul where he died in 1897.[49] In other words, despite the fact that Isma'il was an immigrant, his sons were integrated into the Ottoman hierarchy of the later Tanzimat period, a sign perhaps of the respect that the Ottoman establishment cherished for shaykh Isma'il.

CONCLUSION

Nothing written by shaykh Isma'il al-Shirwani has reached us, but he was the first emissary to carry the Khalidiyya into Daghestan. Despite the relatively short time that he spent in propagating the teachings of the sub-order there, his mission met with instant success and animated the people of these regions with a new vision which came to combat religious and moral laxity and helped to unite the various tribes in a long struggle against Russian domination.

Indeed, the primary goal of spreading the Khalidiyya in Daghestan was the enforcement of the *shari'a* in public life and the bringing of spiritual revival into the Muslim communities there, not to arouse *jihad*. The resort to *jihad* came after the Russian annexation of those regions. There is nothing to show that it was initiated by Shirwani himself. No source available to us attributes that to him. In fact he was already out of the country when it started. As understood by the followers of the sub-order, Khalidi teachings left them no choice but the path of holy war, carried out as is well known by the Murid movement which was initially organized by Isma'il's successors.

Little is known of Shirwani's activity in his new habitat in central Anatolia. Khalidi sources concentrate on the first period of his life and work, and Ottoman sources seem to have ignored him. It is not sure that he established a *zawiya* in Amasya. The allowance provided to him by the treasury was hardly sufficient for his own expenses, and his mausoleum and the mosque that carries his name were built by his son Mehmed Rushdi Pasha in 1869–70, after that he reached a high position in Istanbul. When the ex-mufti of Baghdad Mahmud Shihab al-Din al-Alusi passed through Amasya on his way back to his own country, he was accommodated at the house of Ahmet Hulusi, Shirwani's son. But, when he recorded that, Alusi did not even refer to his host's father, shaykh Isma'il, who had passed away only a few years before, though he did refer to the shaykh's son-in-law, 'Isa al-Shirwani, as the leading scholar in the town.[50] At all events, Shirwani's sojourn there seems to have attracted many immigrants from Shirvan, a number of whom apparently became his followers. He ordained only a few deputies from among them. One of them was his son-in-law, another was Hamza Nigari who succeeded him and kept his line alive for the next generation.[51] But shaykh Isma'il is still remembered in the Caucasus, as a short biography about him published recently (2003) in Azeri Turkish shows.[52]

However, the *silsila* of his deputy Khas Muhammad survived the Russian persecution. One of its followers, shaykh Abdullah al-Daghestani, after staying in Bursa for some years, immigrated to Damascus in about 1925. There, he trained shaykh Nazim al-Qubrusi, the founder of the Haqqaniyya branch of the order which is currently active especially among the members of Muslim communities in several western countries.[53]

APPENDIX

[Khalid's letter to Isma'il al-Shirwani]

From the humble servant (i.e. Khalid) ... to Shaykh Isma'il ... loyalty and honour compel you to come sometimes and meet us ... or to write. There are [many] of our servants [i.e. deputies] who live further than you do. They are older in their association and have performed more services [to us than you]. But still they do not act without our permission... [In this order] the leading shaykh is an intermediary (*wasita*) between the *murid* and his God. Thus, avoiding him [means] avoiding Him. [Consequently] do not train anyone to link with your image and if it appears to him it is an act of the Satan. Do not ordain any deputy except by my [explicit] order... If you continue to disregard [our directions] ... we shall turn away from you completely... You have been warned.

(undated)

NOTES

1   On the treaty of Gulestan see J.C. Hurewitz, *The Middle East and North Africa in World Politics* (New Haven, 1975), vol.1, pp. 197-99.

2   On these events see John F. Baddeley, *The Russian Conquest of the Caucasus,* repr. with a foreword by Moshe Gammer (London, 1999), pp. 123-51; Anna Zelkina, *In Quest for God and Freedom* (London, 2000), pp. 69ff.

3   Nadhir al-Durgili, *Nuzhat al-Adhhan fi Tarajim 'Ulama' Daghestan,* ed. by Michael Kemper and Amri R. Sixsaidov (Berlin, 2004).

4   *Ibid.*, pp. 43ff. for shaykh Sa'id al-Harakani, and pp. 54ff. for Muhammad al-Yaraghi.

5   For a biography of shaykh Isma'il see Mahmud Kemal Inal, *Son Sadrıazamlar* (Istanbul, 1940), I, 436, n. 1; Hüseyin Vassaf, *Sefine-i Evliya,* vol. 2, hazırlayan: Ali Yılmaz ve Mehmet Akkuş (Istanbul, 1999), pp. 371-73; and Fariz Xalilli, *Movlana Ismayil Siraceddin Şirvani Hayati, Faaliyyati, va Ardicillari* (Baku, 2003).

6   Vassaf, II, 371; Xalilli, 27.

7   It is not clear how he could have performed the pilgrimage in 1227/(December) 1812. No organized caravans left for the Hijaz in that year because it was still under the Wahhabis. Shirwani must have gone without the traditional Ottoman service. However, Mecca fell back into the hands of the army of Muhammad 'Ali on 15 January 1813.

8   On Shaykh Abdullah al-Dihlawi see Abd al-Majid al-Khani, *al-Hada'iq al-Wardiyya* (Cairo, 1308), pp. 209ff; C.W. Troll, *Sayyid Ahmad Khan* (New Delhi, 1978), pp. 30ff.

9   Vassaf, II, p. 372; Xalilli, p. 27.

10   *Ibid.*, p. 31; Vassaf, II, p. 372.

11   M.K. Inal, *Son Sadrıazamlar,* I, p. 436 n. 1. For a photo of the *levha* see Xalilli, opposite p. 42.

12   For the period he spent with shaykh Khalid see Xalilli, p. 31.

13   On the practice of *suhba* in the Khalidi sub-order see M. ibn Sulayman, *al-Hadiqa al-Nadiyya,* on the margin of Ibn Sanad, *Asfa al-Mawarid min silsal ahwal al-Imam Khalid* (Cairo, 1313), p. 86. Cf. Muhammad al-Khani, *al-Bahja al-Saniyya* (Cairo, 1303), pp. 30f.

14   See my '*Khalwa* and *Rabita* in the Khalidi Suborder', in Marc Gaborieau et al., *Naqshbandis* (Istanbul-Paris, 1990), pp. 289-302.

15   Ibn Sulayman, p. 80; Makhmudbekov, 'Miuridicheskaia sekta na Kavkaza', *Sbornik materialov dlia opisaniia mestnostei i plemen Kavkaza,* XXIV (1898), p. 23. I am grateful to M. Gammer for a copy of this article and to Dr. Arkadi Purisman of the University of Haifa for his help in translating it. For the *Ijazetname* see Xalilli, pp. 32-4.

16   Makhmudbekov, p. 23.

17   On shaykh 'Uthman Tawila see Ferhad Shakley, 'The Naqshbandi Shaykhs of Hawraman and the Heritage of Khalidiyya-Mujaddidiyya in Kurdistan' in Elizabeth Özdalga (ed.), *Naqshbandis in Western and Central Asia* (Istanbul, 1999), pp. 89-100.

18   Alexander Bennigsen and S. Enders Wimbush, *Mystics and Commissars: Sufism in the Soviet Union* (London, 1985), p. 18 and n. 23; see also M. Gammer, 'The Beginnings of the Naqshbandiyya in Daghestan and the Russian Conquest of the Caucasus', *Die Welt des Islams,* XXXIV, 2, 1994, pp. 206-07 and n. 8; Zelkina, pp. 58ff.

19   Bennigsen and Wimbush, pp. 18f., and n. 22.

20   *Ibid.*; Alexander Bennigsen, 'Un mouvement populaire au Caucase du XVIIIe siècle : La "guerre sainte" du Shaykh Mansur (1785–1794', *Cahiers du monde russe et soviétique,* V, 2, 1964, pp. 159-205. See p. 176, n. 2 where Bennigsen cites Hasaev; see also Zelkina, p. 66.

21   Bennigsen and Wimbush, p. 19.

22   M. Gammer, *Muslim Resistance to the Tsar: Shamil and the Conquest of Chechnia and Daghestan* (London, 1994), p. 6.

23   John F. Baddeley, *The Russian Conquest of the Caucasus* (repr. London, 1999), pp. 58, 139; Xalilli, p. 38.

24   Gammer, *Muslim Resistance*, p. 41.

25   Al-Durgili, *Nuzhat al-Adhhan*, p. 48.

26   Yohanan Friedmann, *Shaykh Ahmad Sirhindi* (Montreal, 1971), p. 68.

27   See my *Studies on Islam and the Ottoman Empire in the 19th Century 1826–1876* (Istanbul, 2001), pp. 22ff.

28   Baddeley, p. 234.

29   Xalilli, p. 41.

30   Zelkina, pp. 102-07; al-Durgili, p. 55; Xalilli, pp. 41-5.

31   Baddeley, pp. 234, 237.

32   See the section 'The Teachings of the Naqshbandiyya-Khalidiyya' in my *Studies on Islam*, pp. 22ff.

33   Makhmudbekov, *Muslim Resistance,* p. 22.

34   Gammer, *Muslim Resistance*, p. 34; *EI2,* IX, p. 487.

35   Xalilli, pp. 38-45; Baddeley, p. 234; Makhmudbekov, p. 23.

36   Vassaf, II, p. 372; cf. Baddeley, p. 234 and Gammer, *Muslim Resistance*, pp. 39-40.

37   For the Sufi chain (*silsila*) of shaykh Isma'il in Daghestan and Chechnya see Jamal al-Din al-Daghistani al-Ghazi-Ghum qi, *al-Adab al-Marziyya fi al-Tariqa al-Naqshbandiyya* (St. Petersburg, 1905), pp. 80-1.

38   J. McCarthy, *Muslims and Minorities: The Population of Ottoman Anatolia and the End of the Empire* (New York, 1983), p. 2; Kemal H. Karpat, *Ottoman Population 1830–1914* (Madison, 1985), pp. 57, 65ff.; Ahmet Cevat Eren, *Turkiye'de Goç ve Goçmen Meseleleri* (Istanbul, 1966), pp. 38, 63ff.

39   Ahmet Rasim, *Osmanlı Tarihi*, vol. 4 (Istanbul, 1328), pp. 1861-62.

40   Xalilli, pp. 46-7 and n. 19.

41   Ibn Sulayman, 80; Abdiolu Husameddin Yaşar, *Amasya Tarihi*, 5 vols., vol. 1, p. 202.

42   Başbakanlık Osmanlı Arşivi, Dahiliyye Iradeleri, no. 446.

43   *Ibid.*, no. 446/3.

44   Muhammad al-Khani, *al-Bahja al-Saniyya*, pp. 44-5; and my article (n. 14 above), pp. 296ff. For the text of the letter see M. As'ad Sahibzade, *Bughyat al-Wajid fi Maktubat Hadrat Mawlana Khalid* (Damascus, 1334/1915–16), pp. 174-77; for a translation see Appendix here.

45   Ibn Sulayman, p. 80; *Amasya il Yilligi* (Amasya, 1967), p. 192.

46   M.K. Inal, *Son Sadrıazamlar,* vol. 1, pp. 436ff.; Ahmed Lutfi, *Vak'a-Nuvis Ahmed Lutfi Efendi Tarihi,* C.XV (Ankara, 1993), p. 110.

47   Mahmud Celaluddin, *Mir'at-i Hakikat,* 3 vols. (Der Saadet, 1326), vol. 1, p. 92.

48   On Ahmed Hulusi see 'Türk Diyanet Vakfi', *Islam Ansiklopedisi,* vol. 2 (Istanbul, 1989), p. 90; 'Sicilli Osmani', vol. 1, p. 307.

49   Xalilli, p. 48; Vassaf, II, p. 372.

50   Mahmud Shihab al-Din al-Alusi, *Nashwat al-Mudam fi al-'Awd ila Madinat al-Salam* (Baghdad, 1293), pp. 14-6.

51   On Hamza Nigari see Abdurrahman Memiş, *Halidi Bagdadi … ve Anadoluda Halidilik* (Istanbul, 2000), pp. 166-67; M.K. Inal, Son Asir Türk Şairleri, vol. II (Istanbul, 1969), pp. 1200ff.

52   Fariz Xalilli (n. 5 above).

53   On Nazim al-Qubrusi see Tayfun Atay, *Bati'da Bir Nakşi Cemaati Şeyh Nazim Kibrisi Örneği* (Istanbul, 1996), pp. 72-3; Adnan M. al-Qabbani, *al-Futuhat al-Haqqaniyya* (n.p., n.d.), pp. 283-347.

HASAN AL-ALQADARI:
THE LAST REPRESENTATIVE OF TRADITIONAL
LEARNING IN DAGHESTAN

SONIA CHESNIN

The 19th century was a turning point in the history of Daghestan. For more than thirty years, from the late 1820s until 1859, the mountain dwellers conducted their struggle for independence against Russian encroachment. The last leader of the resistance, the *imam* Shamil, ultimately surrendered, and the country was conquered. Local self-government was abolished and was replaced by direct Russian administration. Daghestan was divided into districts (*okrugi*) and sub-districts (*naibstva*). Military officers were appointed to head each administrative unit. Usually the judges (*qadi*s) and *naib*s (governors of a *naibstvo*) were local people, many of them ex-supporters of Shamil.[1] Daghestan was, thus, torn from its traditional orientation towards the world of Islam and confronted with Russian and more generally Western civilization. However, pacification did not bring peace and quiet. A number of revolts shook Daghestan between the conquest and the Bolshevik Revolution. All of them were brutally suppressed.

It was in this period of transition and turmoil that Daghestan witnessed the appearance of a remarkable personality: Hasan ʿAli Efendi al-Alqadari, an accomplished scholar, an expert on Islamic law and its practice in Daghestan, a historian and a philosopher. His writings include *Kitap Asar-ı Dağıstan* (Baku, 1903) – a comprehensive history of Daghestan; *al-Takhmis* (Istanbul, 1907) – poems on ʿAbd al-Latif Donogono;[2] *Sharh al-Urda al-Mahdiyya* (Temir-Khan-Shura, 1910) – a commentary on *al-Takhmis*; *Jirab al-Mamnun* (Temir-Khan-Shura, 1912) – a collection of al-Alqadari's *fatwa*s given at various times;[3] *Diwan al-Mamnun*[4] (Temir-Khan-Shura, 1913) – a collection of al-Alqadari's poems, written in various periods of his life, amounting in fact to his autobiography; and apparently a *diwan* in his native Lezghin language, which seems not to have survived.[5] At the same time he was a public figure enmeshed in political affairs. Thus, his biography intersected with nearly every aspect of the social, cultural, and political history of Daghestan of his time.

Soviet scholars, quoting Hasan al-Alqadari's works, record the birth, on 11 Jumada al-Thani 1250/15 October 1834, of a son to Hajj 'Abdallah of the Qurban 'Ali family who received the name Hasan. Although originally from the village of Alqadar in the Khanate (later the district) of Kurah (*Kiurinskii okrug*), the family was living at that time in the village of Balakan in the Avar Khanate (later district – *Avarskii okrug*).[6] The reason for this lay in the connections of his family to the resistance movement against Russia and its leaders. Hajj 'Abdallah, Hasan's father, was the favourite disciple of Shaykh Muhammad Hafiz al-Yaraghi, who introduced the Naqshbandiyya-Mujaddidiyya-Khalidiyya into Daghestan and initiated Ghazi Muhammad and Shamil – respectively the first (1830–32) and third (1834–59) leaders of the future resistance. Hasan's mother was Hafisa, Shaykh al-Yaraghi's daughter and the widow of the first *imam* Ghazi Muhammad. Al-Alqadari was thus destined to bear throughout his life the pain and suffering, the ups and downs of what is known in Russian historiography as the "Caucasian war".

Shaykh Muhammad al-Yaraghi's activities in spreading the Khalidiyya, already banned since 1820,[7] in Daghestan were a source of deep concern to the Russian authorities. He was considered by them, and subsequently by Russian and Soviet historiography, as the instigator of the resistance and the founder of a political-religious movement they called "Miuridizm". In consequence, in 1824 they ordered Aslan Khan, the ruler of Kurah, to arrest the Shaykh and to deliver him to Quba. Aslan Khan made an attempt to stop the Shaykh's preaching. He attended a gathering of *mullah*s from various places and entered into a heated debate with the Shaykh. In his rage the Khan hit the Shaykh, ignoring al-Yaraghi's reputation as a prominent scholar and saint. Subsequently the Khan apologized and released the Shaykh on condition that he abstain from disseminating the Naqshbandi *tariqa* and from calling the people to *jihad*.[8]

However, a short while later, in 1825, the Khan was compelled to imprison Muhammad al-Yaraghi again, under pressure from General Yermolov, the notorious Russian governor of the Caucasus. With the assistance of his associates and pupils according to one version, and that of Aslan Khan himself according to another, Shaykh Muhammad al-Yaraghi managed to escape on the very first night of his imprisonment and found refuge in Tabasaran.[9] In 1828, after living in Tabasaran for three years, the Shaykh returned to Kurah. He was immediately arrested and sent with a convoy to Tiflis. However once again he was rescued by his followers. This time, taking his family and library along with him, he passed via Tabasaran to Avaristan where he finally settled in Balakan.[10]

By the time of his arrival Avaristan, Kurah, and other regions of Daghestan were engulfed by armed conflict. Ghazi Muhammad, his disciple and now also son-in-law,[11] proclaimed *jihad* against the Russians with the Shaykh's blessing.[12] The military successes of Ghazi Muhammad against Russian troops and fortifications in Daghestan and Chechnya forced the Russians to adopt drastic measures to suppress the movement and they gathered a huge force to crush the Imam. Ghazi Muhammad failed in his attempt to negotiate with the commanders of this enormous force,[13] and he was killed in an unequal final battle in his native village of Ghimrah on 29 October 1832. *Diwan al-Mamnun* contains an extensive description of Ghazi Muhammad's last battle.[14]

Ghazi Muhammad's death marked a turning point in the life of Hajj 'Abdallah. Very devoted to his master, Hajj 'Abdallah had supported Shaykh Muhammad's escape from Kurah and had followed his teacher to Avaristan.[15] There he had shared all the privations and hardships with the Shaykh.[16] Now, he married Hafisa, Ghazi Muhammad's widow, whom he genuinely loved, and who had been promised to him by her father, Muhammad al-Yaraghi, before her marriage to Ghazi Muhammad.[17]

After Shaykh al-Yaraghi's death, in 1838,[18] Hajj 'Abdallah and his family returned to his native village of Alqadar. His return coincided with *imam* Shamil's victories and the growing development of the resistance movement in Daghestan and Chechnya. Avaristan was not a secure place to stay in. The Kurah region, on the contrary, was relatively quiet. It was only after weighing the pros and cons that he arrived at the decision to return to Alqadar. It is most unlikely, however, that he would have returned, together with his family, to the Kurah district without prior permission from the Russian administration and the local authorities. The local rulers – Muhammad Mirza Khan, Hajji Yusuf Khan (under whom Hasan al-Alqadari would start his administrative career), and Harun Bek – provided him with the necessary conditions for building and opening his *madrasa* (school). With their help and support, augmented by that of the elders of the *jama'a* (community) and the clans, Hajj 'Abdallah opened the *madrasa* and taught there for twenty five years.[19]

Hajj 'Abdallah was recognized as an authority in the *'ulum*, notably in Arabic grammar, logic, mathematics, philosophy, poetry, etc. His knowledge was encyclopaedic. The honourable title of "Efendi", given to him by the local scholars, places Hajj 'Abdallah among the major scholars of Daghestan in the nineteenth century. A great number of *'ulama'*, graduates of his *madrasa*, gained recognition as scholars in their native district of Kurah and far beyond. Hasan al-Alqadari and his younger brothers acquired a great deal of their knowledge in Islamic studies in this *madrasa*.

Hasan al-Alqadari spent his first four years in Avaristan. His mother Hafisa would sing traditional lullabies to him. His grandfather Muhammad would relate Daghestani legends and tales to him. When the child grew older the grandfather began to tell him about the Prophet Muhammad and his deeds. Everything that Hasan al-Alqadari learned at home in his childhood proved useful to him in the future, in his writings and in his pedagogic work.

Hasan al-Alqadari began his education at the age of seven in his father's *madrasa* in Alqadar. It was his father, Hajj 'Abdallah, who taught him to love poetry, to feel the melody of a poem, to express his feelings and thoughts in a clear and accurate way. It was his father who taught Hasan to appreciate life and try to perceive its meaning. Indeed, in his poetry Hasan al-Alqadari always expressed the deepest love and respect for his father, describing the relations of trust between them. He was not only a beloved father to him, but also his first and for many years his only teacher. In an elegy dedicated to his father on his death (in 1862) Hasan al-Alqadari described his personal loss and grief:

(1)   A misfortune befell me,
       And the lot fell upon me,
       What a misfortune! I am sleepless.

(2)   How am I to be consoled after
       The separation from my father,
       A remarkable scholar, a husband
       And a virtuous man?[20]

He followed a long and difficult path in his studies, first in his father's school, then individually with some of the best known scholars of Daghestan and Azerbaijan. This is what he wrote about his education:

... after I grew up I started my education in the madrasa. I pursued Arabic studies there for 15 years. I also studied the Persian and the Turkish languages with Sayyid 'Abdallah Efendi al-Qarakhani. For a period I studied Qur'an with my enlightened uncle Hajj Isma'il Efendi... Later I mastered the textbooks in physics and in philosophy under the guidance of Mirza 'Ali Efendi al-Akhdi. After completing my education I engaged in teaching... I also wanted to leave for Istanbul to continue my studies, but I was compelled to give up this trip because of my father's death and the need to take care of my younger brothers and sisters.[21]

Hasan al-Alqadari describes the long process of his education in just a few sentences. Everything seems to have been simple and easy. In fact it was a long and exhausting effort. The traditional system of education in Daghestan, which had been shaped in the fifteenth century[22] and existed until at least the 1930s, was divided into three stages:

1. Elementary education, i.e., Qur'anic school, lasted for 3-4 years. The educational network of Qur'anic schools embraced almost every social layer of the population. In every village and hamlet in Daghestan there was a mosque school, or groups of 3-15 pupils studying with a *mullah*, a *qadi*, or an old man of some education.[23] If there was no one who could teach in a village, the villagers would "invite such a person from another village for a specific annual salary".[24] A Russian official reported:

If we compare the number of schools with the size of the population, we should come to the conclusion that the Mountain Daghestanis have outstripped even some civilized European nations. Education is accessible for every Mountain boy; ... every mosque has its own school, where everybody searching for knowledge can study.[25]

Pupils in these schools were taught the recitation of the Qur'an and elementary Muslim obligations and rituals as well as mathematics (*hisab*) and geometry (*handasa*). Girls and boys learned separately, the girls being taught by educated women, usually the *mullah*'s or *qadi*'s wife.[26]

2. The secondary school, i.e., the school of *muta'allim*s (disciples), taught some elements of higher Muslim education. These schools existed in every large village of Daghestan. Traditionally every *'alim* could establish such a school. The number of disciples could vary from 2-3 to more than 50. The disciples were given food and housing by the *jama'a* and by prosperous individuals. The instruction was, practically, individual.[27] It is obvious that success in learning depended on the personality and authority of the *'alim*.

85

3. Higher education and specialization. After completing a "high" school every disciple could continue to study with another *'alim* in order to master different branches of learning. Among such famous teachers were, according to a partial list in *Asar-ı Dağıstan*, Sa'id al-Harakani, Shaykh Muhammad al-Yaraghi, Hajj 'Abdallah Efendi al-Alqadari, Hajj Salim Efendi al-Mahmud-Kenti and Hajj 'Ali Efendi al-Ruquni.[28] Hasan al-Alqadari himself studied physics and mathematics with Mirza 'Ali Efendi al-Akhdi and Qur'an with his uncle Hajj Isma'il Efendi.

One result of his traditional education was the fluency in the three classical languages – Arabic, Turkish and Persian – which al-Alqadari demonstrated in his writings. His *Kitap Asar-ı Dağıstan* was written in Turkish. All his other works – *al-Takhmis*, *Sharh al-Urda al-Mahdiyya*, *Diwan al-Mamnun* and *Jirab al-Mamnun* – were written in Arabic. The last two works included many verse passages in Persian. In addition to all this al-Alqadari spoke several local languages fluently.

Al-Alqadari began his administrative career in 1856 as a secretary to one of the local rulers, Hajji Yusuf Khan, and as a tutor to his sons. In the Khan's entourage al-Alqadari was a witness to Shamil's surrender in Ghunib in 1859. Later he was among the Daghestani notables invited to the victory celebration in Tiflis. In 1865 al-Alqadari received his first commission of *junker* (cadet); and was nominated as a member of the District Court; in 1867 he received his commission of *podpraporshchik* (second lieutenant); in 1871 that of *podporuchik* (lieutenant); and in 1874 that of *poruchik* (senior lieutenant). Between 1866 and 1877 he served as *na'ib* in Southern Tabasaran.

In 1866–67 al-Alqadari was at the head of a contingent of local irregulars sent to crush the resistance of the last rebel stronghold in Qaytaq. Ten years later he demonstratively tore off his officer's shoulder straps and was court-martialed for joining the rebels.

The rebellion was violently suppressed in November 1877. Many settlements were levelled to the ground; hundreds of rebels were hanged. Over 3,000 people without distinction of age, sex and degree of guilt were exiled to the inner regions of Russia. Among the exiled was al-Alqadari.

The data that we have at our disposal on the causes of his arrest and exile to the city of Spassk in the region of Tombovsk, where he spent 4 years, are very contradictory. Al-Alqadari's son, the famous Daghestani historian 'Ali Hasanov, interpreted these events in the following way:

Once the rebels of Southern Tabasaran demanded of al-Alqadari that he quit serving Russia and join the revolt, al-Alqadari got into a rage, tore off his shoulder straps and angrily threw them away. This seems to have been his only participation in the revolt.[29]

In his *Diwan al-Mamnun* al-Alqadari gives two explanations for his arrest and exile. First, he did not inform the authorities about the impending revolt.[30] Secondly, he was a victim of intrigues by Russian officials and of slander by malevolent colleagues:

> I was released from the citadel of Derbend thanks to the pledge of General Orbeliani, who had then become the commandant of the fortress of Ghunib. Upon my release I hurried to Ghunib to thank him for his good deed. However my trip to Ghunib evoked the anger and rage of General Komarov, the governor of Derbend. As a matter of fact, there had been hidden hostility and rivalry between those two, of which I was unaware. Moreover, somebody misled me by suggesting the necessity of this trip, indeed for the obvious reason – to turn the General's anger against me. I will not name this shameless deceiver - Allah has just called him. The Governor did his best to include my name in the list of exiles ... [31]

Al-Alqadari's arrest and consequent exile to Siberia[32] served as a line of demarcation in his life and career: the officer who turned against authority could no longer be trusted by it. Therefore, on his return to his native country in June 1883, he had to begin a new career as teacher, writer and judge.

Even before his arrest and exile al-Alqadari believed that the peoples of the Caucasus should awake and follow the road of progress. To do so they had to adapt to the modern world and embrace Western science and technology. It was thanks to science that the European states had succeeded in the various spheres of life, military and others:

> My dear brother, you can not know
>
> Why they achieved such amazing domination:
>
> By science, by science and again by science![33]

Al-Alqadari was in close contact with leading Islamic reform-minded intellectuals in Baku, such as Zerdabi,[34] Quluzadeh,[35] Akhundzadeh,[36] and towards the end of his life Köcherli,[37] and he shared their ideas. That is why he gave an enthusiastic welcome to the newspaper *Ekinji* (*The Ploughman*),[38] contributed to it and tried to spread its ideas among the people of Daghestan. In his contributions to the newspaper he called on his compatriots to put an end to their "centuries old" ignorance and backwardness, to try to understand and adopt Western civilization, because, "misunderstanding this civilization, the mountain dwellers are wandering in the desert of ignorance".[39]

On his return from exile, al-Alqadari restored his father's *madrasa*. However, realizing that the traditional way of learning could not supply responses to the needs of a new age of changes, he looked for new methods of education.[40] Since the 1860s there had been some schools in Temir-Khan-Shura which aimed at spreading literacy in the native languages of Daghestan as a means to establishing modern schools in various Daghestani languages. A Russian official "was witness" in the winter of 1866–1867 "to the very beginning of the successful spreading of literacy in the Avar language in Temir-Khan-Shura".[41] However such activity, while sufficient to spread literacy, was far from enough to supply a base for modern education and replace the traditional schools teaching in Arabic. Hasan al-Alqadari believed, on the contrary, that traditional education should not be destroyed, but should be used as a means to introduce modern education, including local languages as well as Russian.

Connected to this issue was the question of the language of instruction that might serve as a vehicle for modern education. Russian was out of the question, because the Daghestanis both did not know it and were suspicious of schools using it in instruction. The local languages were far from suitable for the task – even their alphabets (based on Arabic, or rather Persian, orthography) had not yet been finally agreed on. The two possible languages were Arabic, which in Egypt and in Lebanon had been developing into a modern vehicle of written communication, and Turkish. In view of the fact that textbooks were easiest to obtain in Baku and indeed were received from there,[42] it seems most probable that the main (though by no means the only) language of instruction was Turkish. This should not have posed major difficulties because the traditional (spoken) *lingua franca* in Daghestan was one Turkish dialect or another.

In addition to the textbooks students in Hasan Efendi's *madrasa* received and used newspapers like *Säda* (*The Voice*)[43] from Baku, *Terjüman/Perevodchik* (*The Translator*)[44] from Bakhchisarai and *al-Mu'ayyad* (*The Victorious*)[45] from Cairo. Sometimes they received also Ottoman newspapers and there is evidence that al-Alqadari received newspapers from Russia also.

Unlike many other schools in Daghestan, al-Alqadari's *madrasa* was a comprehensive institution providing elementary up to higher education. Many students from Azerbaijan, Tiflis, Tatarstan, Daghestan and the northern Caucasus came to study in it. Some of them spoke Persian, Turkish and other languages. These students were used by al-Alqadari to teach their native languages to other students. The oldest students taught the younger ones. Teaching gave students an exemption from tuition fees. This system gave a chance to many talented youngsters from poor backgrounds to complete their education. There were eight classrooms in the *madrasa*, all of them large and with plenty of light. In each there were new desks, a blackboard, a bookshelf, a table for the teacher, chairs. It is known that already in 1884 al-Alqadari asked Hasan Huzunov[46] to prepare for his *madrasa* a globe like those that were in use in Russian schools, though with the difference that the names were to be written in Arabic.[47]

After graduating from al-Alqadari's *madrasa* students could pass the exam in Temir-Khan-Shura, the provincial capital of Daghestan, and receive the diploma of higher Muslim education from the Russian educational authorities.

In his capacity as *qadi* Hasan al-Alqadari explained to his people about the changes that had occurred, trying to help them to adapt to the new circumstances. He answered various questions on Muslim law and its practice in Daghestan. There is evidence that people considered al-Alqadari able to solve any difficulty. Thus his recommendations acquired nearly the strength of a new-style *fatwa*.[48] In his *Jirab al-Mamnun* al-Alqadari used *fatwa*s in order to adapt his people to modern life. Thus, he explained that use of the telegraph does not contradict the Muslim way of life.[49]

Al-Alqadari was very famous and popular throughout Daghestan. His authority spread over every sphere of life and was felt on every social level. Suleiman Stal'skii, a prominent Lezghin poet, whom Gorky called the Homer of the twentieth century, wrote that "with the death of al-Alqadari masters and peasants are weeping".[50]

In folklore he was described as "the head of the Daghestani *'ulama'* and "a bright lamp of science and mind":

> Who will not die for the truth?
> The light of justice has died away.
> Mirza Hasan has passed away.
> A great misfortune has befallen us.[51]

Hasan al-Alqadari was a highly important figure in the intellectual-religious life of the Caucasus from the 1860s to the 1900s. It is not surprising, therefore, that many legends were shaped around his outstanding personality. One of these concerned his mysterious birth. The late N. Nurmahomedov, a traditionally educated Muslim scholar and professor at the University of Islam in Daghestan, recounted in October 1993:

> My teachers Alil Muhammad Hajiyav and his brother Alil Abdulla Hajiyav shared the following information with me: it turns out that al-Alqadari's biological father was Ghazi Muhammad. 'Ali Kayaev, a great expert on Islam, Arabic philology and eastern manuscripts, claimed that he owns a written record by Shaykh Muhammad al-Yaraghi on Hasan al-Alqadari's actual birth date. This record states that on the day of the wedding of Hafisa [al-Yaraghi's daughter and Hasan al-Alqadari's mother – S.Ch.] with Hajj 'Abdallah al-Alqadari, she was in her eighth month of pregnancy. Thus, according to this record Hasan al-Alqadari must have been born some time before his official birthday, that is approximately in 1833.[52]

Nurmahomedov added that after the Caucasian war was over and "peace and quiet" were established in Daghestan a respectable delegation of three well-known scholars, authorized by the jama'a of Ghimrah, paid a visit to al-Alqadari. They turned to him with the following request:

> You are the owner of the inheritance left to you by your father Ghazi Muhammad. Come! The jama'a of Ghimrah is waiting for you! [53]

Nurmahomedov stated that the future *imam* of Daghestan Najm al-Din al-Hutsi (Gotsinskii) and the younger brother of Hasan al-Alqadari, Muhammad, who at that time became the *qadi* of southern Daghestan, were also present at that meeting. Hasan al-Alqadari treated the delegation with due respect and hospitality but refused their request, for obvious reasons.[54]

Another legend connected with the personality of al-Alqadari has to do with the rebellion of 1877, one of the most serious revolts of the north-eastern Caucasus at the end of the nineteenth century. According to this tale, "al-Alqadari in collaboration with his brother-in-law on his wife's side led the mountain dwellers' revolt against the rule of the Tsar".[55] We even find archival sources quoted for this amazing story.[56]

If the first tale can be seen as evidence of an oral tradition surviving in Daghestani educational institutions until today, the second shows the careless attitude of some scholars to archival material. In any case, since no solid evidence can be found one has no choice but to regard both of these tales as mythology and to relate them to Soviet and post-Soviet Daghestani politics rather than to the history of nineteenth-century Daghestan.

In any event, it is not important whose son al-Alqadari was, or whether he was the real leader of the 1877 rebellion or not. What is important is his activity. Since the opening of the Nizamiyya *madrasa* in Tsakhur in 1075,[57] Daghestan had produced a long list of scholars, whose comprehensive knowledge has impressed the entire Muslim world.[58] Hasan al-Alqadari was among the greatest representatives of this centuries old tradition. However, he was also thinking of progress and new ideas. Furthermore, he was not just an armchair scholar, but also a man of action, and as such contributed greatly to the Muslim movement of his day in the Caucasus. As we have seen, he welcomed the first "national" Azerbaijani newspaper, *Ekinji*, and was a prominent early contributor to it. In 1904 he took part in the Caucasian Muslim Council in Tiflis, which brought together Muslim scholars, public and political leaders, and experts on Islam from all over the Caucasus to examine Sunni-Shi'i religious institutions in order to diminish the contradictions between them.[59] In 1909, the 50th anniversary of Shamil's surrender was marked at Ghunib. Unable to participate because of age and ill health, al-Alqadari greeted the participants in a *qasida* especially composed for the occasion:

> I remember past time,
> He who lives long, can see another Life.
> It was narrow for a man to live in the mountains.
> He lived as a beast, closed around.
> Poverty persecuted him.
> His villages were like nests of the eagle.
> Now everything is different – the buildings are huge,
> The streets are wide and people live in tranquillity.[60]

Al-Alqadari responded in his work and action to the socio-political climate of the time, and in so doing reinforced the transformations that were occurring. Since al-Alqadari was active in society and politics, his literary work constituted a response to events and a continuous attempt to reshape them. In Soviet historiography he was called "an enlightener".[61] Since some scholars felt uncomfortable about applying European terminology to a Muslim, Abdullaev tried to search for a compromise and coined the term "Muslim enlightener".[62] Perhaps we might more accurately describe him as a *jadid*-reformer.

NOTES

1   For further details, see *Istoriia Dagestana*, II (Moscow, 1968), p. 123; *Asari-Dagestan. Istoricheskie Svedeniia o Dagestane*, trans. and notes Ali Hasanov (Makhachkala, 1994), p. 124.

2   'Abd al-Latif Donogono al-Hutsi (1851/2–1890/1), a famous *'alim* and Sufi shaykh, the son of Shamil's *na'ib* Donogono Muhammad and elder brother of the future Imam of Daghestan and Chechnya (1920), Najm al-Din al-Hutsi. For his biography, see Mansur Gaidarbekov, 'Abdulatip Gotsinskii', *Akhulgo* (Makhachkala, 1999), No. 3, pp. 36-45.

3   For details, see M.-S. Saidov, 'Gasan Alqadari – vidnyi Dagestanskii uchenyi', in *Istoriko-literaturnoe nasledie Gasana Alkadari* (Makhachkala, 1988), pp. 44-45; for further details on *Jirab al-Mamnun* see chapter by Kemper in this volume.

4   Al-Mamnun was a pen name of al-Alqadari.

5   A.B. Baimurzaev, *Iz istorii obschestvennoi mysli Dagestana vtoroi poloviny XIX veka* (Makhachkala, 1965), p. 62.

6   *Asari-Dagestan*, p. 149; Hasan al-Alqadari, *Diwan al-Mamnun* (Temir-Khan-Shura, 1332 [1913-4]), p. 5.

7   M. Gammer, *Muslim Resistance to the Tsar: Shamil and the Conquest of Chechnia and Daghestan* (London, 1994), pp. 39-40, 43; *Asari-Dagestan*, pp. 111-12, 142; *Diwan al-Mamnun*, p. 5; for the spread of the Naqshbandiyya-Khalidiyya in Daghestan, see chapter by Gammer in this volume.

8   A. Agaev, *Magomed Iaragskii* (Makhachkala, 1994), pp. 107-11; R. Rizvanov, 'Pervyi imam i ego uchitel', *Dagestanskaia Pravda*, 18 September 1993.

9   Agaev, *op. cit.*, pp. 120-21.

10   Ibid., pp. 138-39; *Diwan al-Mamnun*, p. 5 ; *Asari-Dagestan*, pp. 142-43; Rizvanov, *art. cit.*

11   The exact date of Ghazi Muhammad's marriage to Hafisa is unknown. According to one version the marriage took place in August 1831 during Ghazi Muhammad's campaign against Derbend (Agaev, *op. cit.*, pp. 140-41; Rizvanov, *art. cit.*). According to another version, Muhammad al-Yaraghi gave his daughter Hafisa to Ghazi Muhammad when he was studying with her father in the village of Yaragh (ca. 1824–1826; Hadzhi Ali syn Abdul Meleka Efendi, *Skazanie Ochevidtsa o Shamile* (Makhachkala, 1990), p. 15, note 9).

12   Shaykh Muhammad al-Yaraghi declared *jihad* against the Russians in September 1830; Gammer, *op. cit.*, pp. 50; 319, note 9.

13   Ibid., p. 59; *Diwan al-Mamnun*, pp. 60-61; *Asari-Dagestan*, p. 113; Agaev, *op. cit.*, pp. 153-4.

14   *Diwan al-Mamnun*, pp. 60-1.

15   In *Asari-Daghistan* (p. 144) al-Alqadari gives another version: "… even in his youth Hajj 'Abdallah Efendi studied with Hajj Salim Efendi from al-Mahmud-Kenti and with Shaykh Muhammad al-Yaraghi. Then he moved to Avaristan and finished his studies under the supervision of Ghazi Muhammad and Hajj 'Ali Efendi. When Shaykh Muhammad escaped to Avaristan he again came to him and stayed with him".

16   *Diwan al-Mamnun*, p. 5.

17   Interview with N.G. Nurmahomedov, October 1993.

18   Aitberov dates al-Yaraghi's death to 1840: see Gaidarbek Genichutlinsky, *Istoriko-biograficheskie i istoricheskie ocherki*, trans. and comments by T. Aitberov (Makhachkala, 1992), pp. 118-9, note 5. Hasan al-Alqadari dated his grandfather's death in 1838 (*Asari-Dagestan, op. cit.*, p. 143; *Diwan al-Mamnun, op. cit.*, p. 5). Agaev gives 1839 as the year of al-Yaraghi's death (*op. cit.*, p. 190).

19   *Asari-Dagestan*, p. 144.

20   *Diwan al-Mamnun*, p. 71.

21   Ibid., pp. 5, 53; *Asari-Dagestan*, p. 149.

22   *Istoriia Dagestana*, p. 112; G. Gamzatov, *Literatura narodov Dagestana dooktiabr'skogo perioda. Tipologiia i svoeobrazie khudozhestvennogo opyta* (Moscow, 1982), p. 61.

23   *Istoriia Dagestana*, p. 346.

24   'Vospominaniia mutalima, Abdully Omar-ogly', *Sbornik svedenii o Kavkazskikh gortsakh*, Vyp. I (Tiflis, 1868), Part VII, p. 20.

25   P. Uslar 'O rasprostranenii gramotnosti mezhdu gortsami', *Sbornik svedenii o Kavkazskikh gortsakh*, Vyp. III (Tiflis, 1870), p. 3.

26   For details on elementary education in Daghestan, see 'Vospominaniia mutalima', *op. cit.*, pp. 15-7.

27   About the ways of life and process of learning of the *muta'allim*s, see ibid., pp. 22-5.

28   *Asari-Dagestan*, pp. 137-50.

29   bid., p. 167, note 162.

30   *Diwan al-Mamnun*, pp. 140-1.

31   Ibid., p. 125.

32   For his activities in exile and its influence on him see chapter by Kemper in this volume.

33   *Diwan al-Mamnun*, p. 204.

34   Hasan Bey Melikov-Zerdabi (1832–1907), one of the leading figures of the Azeri cultural renaissance in the second half of the nineteenth century, best known as the founder and editor of the newspaper *Ekinji*.

For further details see T. Swietochowski and B.C. Collin, *Historical Dictionary of Azerbaijan* (Lanham, Maryland and London, 1999), pp. 134-5. For *Ekinji* see note 38 below.

35 Mammad (Muhammad) Jalal Quluzadeh (1860?–1932), a prominent writer and journalist, best known as the founder and editor of the famous satirical journal *Molla Nasreddin*. For further details see ibid., pp. 107-8. For *Molla Nasreddin*, see Alexandre Bennigsen and Chantale Lemercier-Quelquejay, *La presse et le mouvement national chez les musulmans de Russie avant 1920* (Paris, 1964), pp. 124-8.

36 Mirza Fath 'Ali Akhundzadeh (Akhundov; 1812–1871), an outstanding writer and philosopher claimed by both Azerbaijan and Iran as part of their heritage. He is regarded in Azerbaijan as the founder and foremost representative of modern Azeri literature. For further details see Swietochowski and Collin, *op. cit.*, p. 13.

37 Feridun Bey Köcherli, a younger contemporary of al-Alqadari, famous writer and publicist, contributed to *Terjüman/Perevodchik* and to *Sharq-i Russ*. Best known for his monumental multi-volume *Literatura Azerbaidzhanskikh Tiurkov*, which he composed in the early 1900s.

38 Published three times a week between 1875 and 1877 by Hasan Bey Melikov-Zerdabi, this was the first Turkic Muslim periodical approved by the Russian censorship. For further details see Bennigsen and Lemercier-Quelquejay, *op. cit.*, pp. 27-30.

39 *Ekinji*, 1875, No. 8.

40 Soviet and post-Soviet Daghestani scholars have tended to exaggerate the reformist, "secular" and "progressive" views and activities of al-Alqadari. Thus, it has been claimed that he and Hasan Zerdabi were thinking of establishing a secular (*sic!*) school in Daghestan; see M. Abdullaev, 'Mesto i rol' Gasana Alkadari v istorii dukhovnoi kul'tury narodov dorevoliutsionnogo Dagestana', in *Istoriko-literaturnoe nasledie, op. cit.*, pp. 11-2. It is much more likely that al-Alqadari intended reforms in the traditional educational system. Abdullaev also claims that al-Alqadari founded the first secular school in Daghestan with a learning process conducted in the Azerbaijani language; see M. Abdullaev, *Iz istorii, op. cit.*, p. 13. He states that the central topic of study in al-Alqadari's *madrasa* was the achievements of Arab and European sciences, and especially the latest innovations in agriculture or handicrafts. After graduating from the school the students supported the introduction of these innovations in their native villages; ibid., *loc. cit.* On reading these lines of Abdullaev it seemed to me that al-Alqadari's *madrasa* should be called an industrial school, but this in no way fits the reality. For obvious reasons al-Alqadari's *madrasa* could not be a secular school on the pattern of Russian or European institutions. It was, most probably, some kind of symbiosis of the traditional Muslim school with borrowings from the schools of Russia.

41 Uslar, *art. cit.*, p. 25

42 S. Hajjiev 'Riq'el hkunar' (unpublished memoirs kept in the private collection of Kurban Akimov, whose older brother studied in al-Alqadari's *madrasa*), pp. 89, 90, 95, 97. I am grateful to Mr. Akimov for allowing me to study the memoirs; *Asari-Dagestan*, p. 169, note 198. *Diwan al-Mamnun*, pp. 181-82; *Istoriko-literaturnoe nasledie Gasana Alkadari, op. cit.*, pp. 137-8.

43 Published first three times a week and later daily between 1909 and 1911 by Hashim Bey Vezirov, and closed down because of "Pan-Islamism". It continued publication under various names until 1915. For the periodical see Bennigsen and Lemercier-Quelquejay, *op. cit.*, p. 114. For Vezirov see ibid., p. 112. Some sources state that *Ekinji* was also received there. This must be a misunderstanding: al-Alqadari's students could not receive *Ekinji* for the simple reason that the newspaper stopped publication in 1877, while the *madrasa* was opened only after al-Alqadari's return from exile in 1883.

44 The most famous Muslim periodical to be published in Russia, a bilingual weekly published between 1 [13] August 1883 and 23 February 1918 by Ismail Bey Gaspirali/Gasprinskii until his death in 1914, and then by Hasan Sabri Ayvaz (until March 1917), Ismail Bey's daughter, Shefika, and his son Rifat in succession. For further details of the weekly and its famous editor and publisher, see ibid., especially pp. 35-42, 138-40, 247.

45 The most popular daily in Egypt (1889–1915), published and edited by 'Ali Yusuf until his death in 1913. Openly pan-Islamic and anti-British, it enjoyed the support of the *khadivs* Tawfiq (1878–1892) and 'Abbas Hilmi (1892–1914). For further details, see Ami Ayalon, *The Press in the Arab Middle East* (New York, 1995) pp. 57-9, 234-6.

46 Hasan Huzunov (1854–1940) was a famous Daghestani scholar and poet. His philosophical-astronomical treatise *Jawahir al-Buhur* was popular among Daghestani scholars. For further details on Huzunov see M. Abdullaev, *Iz istorii filosofskoi i obschestvenno-politicheskoi mysli narodov Dagestana v 19 v.* (Moscow, 1968), pp. 260-319.

47 *Istoriko-literaturnoe nasledie Gasana Alkadari. Sbornik nauchnykh trudov* (Makhachkala, 1988), pp. 140-1.

48 Abdullaev, *Iz istorii, op. cit.*, p. 13.

49 For further details see chapter by Kemper in this volume.

50 Quoted from Abdullaev, *Iz istorii, op. cit.*, p. 13.

51 E. Emin, *Stikhotvoreniya* (Moscow, 1959), p. 79.

52 Interview with Nurmahomedov, October 1993.

53 Ibid.

54 Ibid.

55 See, for example, Abdullaev, *Iz Istorii, op. cit.*, p. 216, note 4.

56 Rukopisnyi Fond Instituta Istorii Dagestanskogo Filiala Rossiisi Akademii Nauk, document No. 1517. But

when, impressed by this "explosive" material, I started to search for it in different archives, I found nothing. Later, in private conversations, Professor Shikhsaidov told me that he had found in the archives in Tiflis a list of exiled Daghestani notables, with al-Alqadari among them. One can also find the list in al-Alqadari's *Diwan al-Mamnun*, pp. 141-2. These notables were arrested and exiled to Russia for one reason only – their failure to inform the Russian administration about the coming revolt.

57 A.N. Genko, 'Arabskii iazyk i Kavkazovedenie', *Trudy vtoroi sessii assotsiatsii arabistov* (Moscow and Leningrad, 1941), pp. 93-100; G. Ibragimov, 'Khristianstvo u Tsakhurov', *Al'fa i Omega* (Moscow), 1999, No. 1, p. 177.

58 I.Iu. Krachkovskii, 'Dagestan i Iemen', in id., *Izbrannye Sochineniya* (Moscow and Leningrad, 1960), VI, p. 610.

59 F. Köcherli, *Literatura Azerbaidzhanskikh Tiurkov* (Baku, 1981), II, p. 337.

60 Quoted by Saidov, 'Gasan Alkadari', *op. cit.*, p. 46.

61 F. Vagabova, 'Prosvetitel'skaia kontseptsiia lichnosti v tvorchestve Alkadari', in *Istoriko-literaturnoe nasledie Gasana Alkadari*, pp. 68-74; E. Kassiev, 'O nekotorykh prosvetitel'skikh protivorechiyakh v tvorchestve Gasana Alkadari', ibid., pp. 108-11; M. Abdullaev, *Obshchestvenno-politicheskaya mysl*, *op. cit.*, pp. 120, 125.

62 Ibid., pp. 121-7.

DAGHESTANI SHAYKHS AND SCHOLARS IN RUSSIAN EXILE: NETWORKS OF SUFISM, *FATWAS* AND POETRY

MICHAEL KEMPER

After the Russian subjugation of the North Caucasian Imamate (1828–59) and especially after the failure of the rebellion of 1877, thousands of Daghestanis left their home country. Many families performed the *hijra* to the Ottoman Empire where they built up important diaspora groups. At the same time the Russian government forced many mountain dwellers to move to inner Russian provinces where the authorities hoped to keep them under tight control.

My aim is a preliminary investigation into the role of Russian exile in the development of Daghestani Muslim culture. In spite of all the hardships of exile, some Daghestanis seized the opportunity to establish new contacts in their place of banishment – to be sure not with Russians in the first place, but with representatives of other Muslim peoples of the Russian Empire, especially Volga Tatars. The Daghestanis built up new networks which enabled them to overcome the isolation they had suffered from previously, for during the Caucasian War the lands of the Imamate had been under Russian blockade. Furthermore, new contacts with Muslims in Russia also provided new incentives for the development of Sufism and Islamic law in Daghestan itself. We shall take a look at several examples of this development.

I

To be expelled from one's homeland was surely one of the greatest disgraces a Daghestani could think of. In North Caucasian customary law, exile was the traditional punishment for severe offences which required blood revenge, especially murder and rape.[1] Only by leaving the village could the offender (and, in many regions, his nearest relatives) avoid immediate retaliation at the hands of the victim's family, and only after an arrangement involving the payment of blood-money and the granting of pardon from the victim's side would the offender be able to return to his community. To be exiled meant not only to lose the social and economical protection of one's kin group and community; it also meant the loss of any judicial protection.

Therefore it should not come as a surprise that exile to Russia used to have a crushing effect on Daghestanis. In a recent article, Austin Jersild studied Russian archival materials on the fate of some 5,000 primarily Daghestani mountaineers who were banished to different regions in Russia after the North Caucasian rebellion of 1877-78. Daghestani as well as Chechen and Cherkes families were brought mainly to Saratov and Astrakhan provinces in the Middle and Lower Volga region. These regions were inhabited by a mixed population of Slavic origin as well as by Tatars, Bashkirs, and Kazakhs. The exile programs' brought the populations of entire Daghestani villages to the Volga where the mountaineers were forced to build new settlements which bore names like 'Little Daghestan'. Yet the Daghestanis stubbornly refused to work on the fields that had been assigned to them, and fell into complete apathy. In addition, they suffered heavily from diseases so that their number decreased at a terrible rate. It turned out that this type of exile was equivalent to capital punishment. After only a few years, in 1883, the Government had to abandon the project of mass resettlement and to remove the remaining Daghestanis back to the Caucasus.[2]

Alongside this mass exile of entire village populations there was also a type of individual exile to Russia. In the 19th and early 20th centuries (in fact, at least until the 1930s), many prominent Daghestanis were banished to Russian towns or villages, alone or with their families. Their status must have been similar to that of Russian political exiles as they were kept not in prison but under more or less permanent police control.

Daghestani Arabic literature provides many examples of Muslim Sufis and scholars who were sentenced to live in Russia for a certain spell of time. No doubt, the most famous political exile was the third Imam Shamil himself. The Arabic writings of Shamil's son-in-law 'Abd al-Rahman al-Ghazi-Ghumuqi, who accompanied the Imam into exile, describe how the traditionally educated mountaineers perceived modern Russia with all her technical achievements. Yet Shamil's public exposition and touring in Russia and his princely house arrest in Kaluga served above all the celebration of Russia's victory, and it is hard to estimate to what degree Shamil's experience in Russia was somehow conveyed to Daghestanis at home. It is not by chance that 'Abd al-Rahman's Arabic book *Khulasat al-Tafsil* was written not for a Daghestani public, but at Russian request.[3]

It is common knowledge that Shamil's *jihad* as well as the Daghestani rebellion of 1877 had been backed by several *shaykh*s of the Naqshbandiyya-Khalidiyya Sufi order.[4] In order to isolate these 'unruly elements' from their Daghestani communities, the Russian government banished some leading *shaykh*s of the Khalidiyya to the Volga region. Designated as an instrument of repression, this exile paradoxically enabled the Daghestani *shaykh*s to expand their *tariqa* networks into Inner Russia. This can be illustrated by the example of Shaykh Ilyas al-Tsudaqari (d. 1904 or 1908)[5] from the Darghin town of Tsudakhar. He was sent to the Alti Ata valley in Samara province where he enjoyed much respect from the Tatar Muslim population, as his correspondence with local *mullah*s shows.[6] In the new milieu he continued to educate *murid*s and to write Sufi literature, and his most important book appeared in Kazan in the Middle Volga region.[7]

Another prominent case is Shaykh Mahmud al-Almali from the region of Jar and Belokan (in what is today Northern Azerbaijan).[8] Mahmud was exiled to the Volga region twice, and both spells of banishment proved to be very important for the spread of his Naqshbandiyya-Khalidiyya branch. Apparently Mahmud had been working as a secretary for Daniyal, the Sultan of the Daghestani principality of Ilisu (now in Northern Azerbaijan) who at first cooperated with the Russians but then joined Shamil in 1844. Mahmud's connection to Daniyal may have been the reason for his first exile to the province of Perm in the Urals.[9] During this exile in the middle of the 19th century, Mahmud also visited the city of Kazan. Apparently he obtained his initiation into the Khalidiyya brotherhood in Kazan, at the hands of another Daghestani *shaykh* in exile.[10] After his return to the Caucasus, Mahmud began to spread his Khalidiyya link not only in his home region of Jar and Belokan in the South Caucasus, but also to *murid*s from the Samur region of southern Daghestan, and within some decades Mahmud's branch (which soon became labelled the Khalidiyya-Mahmudiyya) also gained a foothold in the central and northern regions of Daghestan. Towards the end of his life, Shaykh Mahmud was once again sent into exile, this time to the city of Astrakhan in the Volga delta. Again we do not know the reason for this banishment, for there is no sign of any anti-government activity on his part. In general, the Mahmudiyya *shaykh*s were known for their clear anti-*jihad* position, and Mahmud's *khalifa*s in Daghestan became the main rivals of the pro-*jihad* Naqshbandiyya group around the Avar *shaykh* 'Abd al-Rahman al-Thughuri (from Sogratl, d. 1882) and his followers. At all events, during his second exile in Astrakhan Mahmud continued to establish further links by initiating new *murid*s into the *tariqa*.

In Astrakhan, shortly before his death in Muharram 1294 (late January 1877),[11] Mahmud gave an *ijaza* to Muhammad-Dhakir al-Chistawi from the town of Chistopol in Tatarstan (d. 1310/1892–93).[12] This al-Chistawi was to become a major protagonist of the Khalidiyya in the Volga-Urals and win many adherents from different regions. Interestingly, at the end of the 19th century another Daghestani shaykh of the Khalidiyya-Mahmudiyya, Sayfallah al-Nitsubkri al-Ghazi-Ghumuqi (d. 1338/1920) from the town of Kumukh in central Daghestan, went to Tatarstan to study with al-Chistawi.[13] When Sayfallah obtained an *ijaza* from al-Chistawi and returned to Daghestan, the way of the Mahmudiyya *silsila* had completed a circle between Tatarstan and the North Caucasus.[14]

As we have seen, sometimes it remains unclear why the Russian administration sent Daghestani *shaykh*s into exile, and it seems that by no means every banishment was caused by political or even anti-governmental activities. This is also evident from the later fate of Sayfallah al-Ghazi-Ghumuqi. After his return to Daghestan, he began to work in Russian service as an official *qadi* for Muslims in the Russian town of Temir-Khan-Shura. Probably around 1912, Sayfallah Qadi was himself exiled to Astrakhan. His own letters to other Mahmudiyya *shaykh*s indicate that this exile resulted from some kind of internal intrigue within the Russian colonial administration. In 1915 Sayfallah was released and returned to his homeland,[15] where he resumed his work in the official Muslim judicial apparatus. His letters show that he continued to be an opponent of *jihad*, and that he even engaged in polemics against the Shaykh Najm al-Din al-Hutsi (Gotsinskii) who was to become one of the main *jihad* leaders in the early 1920s in Daghestan.[16]

Nonetheless Sayfallah's short spell of exile in Astrakhan had a serious effect on Sufi culture in Daghestan. During his exile Sayfallah made the acquaintance of a certain Shaykh Salih b. 'Abd al-Khaliq al-Hanafi who boasted not only a Naqshbandiyya affiliation but also an initiation into the North African Shadhiliyya brotherhood (via links from Istanbul, Medina and Fes in Morocco).[17] In Astrakhan this *shaykh* initiated Sayfallah into the Shadhiliyya and gave him an *ijaza*. When Sayfallah was released from exile and returned to Daghestan in 1915, he promoted not only the Naqshbandiyya-Khalidiyya-Mahmudiyya as he had already done before but also this Moroccan Shadhiliyya branch. In due course, Sayfallah and other Mahmudiyya *shaykh*s like Hasan al-Qahi (d. 1937) developed a curious dual Khalidiyya-Shadhiliyya identity, for they began to practise the vocal *dhikr* of the Shadhiliyya for a larger public and the traditional silent *dhikr* of the Khalidiyya to their most qualified and intimate *murid*s.[18]

These examples indicate that in the late 19th and early 20th centuries, Astrakhan in particular was a melting pot for Sufi *tariqa*s from all over the Russian Empire and beyond. Exile in the Volga region enabled the Daghestani Sufis to make new acquaintances and obtain new initiations. Contacts made in exile in Kazan and Astrakhan were important not only for the emergence of the Khalidiyya-Mahmudiyya, but also for the introduction of the Shadhiliyya to Daghestan where it had hitherto clearly been unknown. Together with the Qadiriyya brotherhood,[19] these *tariqa*s led to important changes in the Daghestani Sufi milieu, especially as they challenged the strong position of the pro-*jihad* faction of the Khalidiyya which had emerged before and during the Imamate.

II

Not only in the sphere of Sufism did exile produce new contacts and networks which were to have a definite impact on the religious culture at home in Daghestan. The example of the Daghestani scholar Hasan al-Alqadari shows that experiences of exile and contacts with Muslims in Russia influenced the development of Islamic law in Daghestan as well.

Hasan al-Alqadari (1834–1910) was a grandson of one of the most famous Khalidiyya *shaykh*s of the *jihad* era, Muhammad al-Yaraghi (d. probably in 1838). Yet no Sufi activity is reported from al-Alqadari himself; rather, he obtained a thorough education in classical *madrasa* sciences and especially in Shafi'i *fiqh* with his father and other scholars from southern Daghestan, and for a short period he even studied astronomy with the poet and notorious opponent of Shamil, Mirza 'Ali al-Akhti. Hasan al-Alqadari then began a career in the Russian administration of Daghestan which brought him to the rank of First Lieutenant (Russ. *poruchik*) and to the position of governor or *naib* (Arab. *na'ib*) of the district of Southern Tabasaran in 1866. On the occasion of the Daghestani revolt of 1877, he reportedly fell victim to an intrigue orchestrated by a rival of Count Orbelianov, al-Alqadari's Russian patron. Accused of having sympathies with the rebellion, al-Alqadari was dismissed and even imprisoned for seven months in Derbend. Finally he was exiled to Russia in 1879. Together with his family he settled in the town of Spassk-Riazanskii (*guberniia* of Tambov) to the south of Moscow. In 1883 he was allowed to move to Astrakhan because of the better climate there, and in the same year he obtained an imperial pardon and returned to his homeland. The exile marked a major break in his life and the end of his career in Russian service. For the following twenty seven years al-Alqadari worked as head of the *madrasa* in his native village of Alqadar in the region of Kura, southern Daghestan, where he died in 1910.[20]

Hasan al-Alqadari is best known for his Turkish sketch of Daghestani history *Athar-i Daghistan* which is especially valuable for its biographical materials on Daghestani scholars.[21] Yet for our purpose two other books of al-Alqadari are more interesting: these are a collection of his poems and a volume of his *fatwas*.

Al-Alqadari's poetic heritage in Arabic is his *Diwan al-Mamnun* (published posthumously in Temir-Khan-Shura in 1913).[22] It not only contains al-Alqadari's poems which he dedicated to friends or wrote for special social occasions but also the grateful responses of his various addressees, also in Arabic poetry; all in all some 90 acquaintances and correspondents are mentioned by name. As the poems are chronologically arranged, the whole book constitutes a kind of poetical autobiography.[23] The poems reflect al-Alqadari's relationship to his friends and teachers, his entry to office, his dismissal, imprisonment and exile as well as numerous occasional meetings; it also gives accounts of his religious convictions, especially of his sympathies for the Family of the Prophet and his contacts with Shi'i scholars – contacts that he was obviously much criticized for by Sunnis. As for al-Alqadari's exile, his poems enable us to trace his travels and meetings in Inner Russia, especially his close relations with Tatar *mullah*s in the villages near his place of settlement.[24]

Besides containing information on al-Alqadari's own exile in Russia, the *Diwan* also presents some poems which other Daghestanis in exile sent to al-Alqadari. For instance an old friend of al-Alqadari, Aqa Mirza al-Qa'ani, wrote him an emotional *qasida* describing the suffering and hopelessness of Daghestani exiles (Arab. *al-usara'*, lit. "prisoners") as he had seen for himself in Saratov province. I quote from this poem which dates from around 1881:

> I was upset when I saw
> the prisoners who hoped to return [to their homeland],
> And who refused what the Treasury
> had assigned to them of money and property. [...]
> The judges in Saratov
> were angry at us in their rage.
> Therefore they shut the door of compassion
> and had us taste the punishment
> By letting us starve and forbidding us to leave
> to [other] regions of the Earth. [...]
> Some prisoners were happy to take the land [they were allotted],

yet they only began to indulge in drinking.
  O how hard did Fate hit the prisoners,
    and indeed, it struck them with strange things.
  Woe! That's what I say to what befell us,
    the afflictions that deprive us of our youth.
  How many of us are hungry and weep
    and wail in their weakness.
  How many of us are naked and barefooted
    and wish they had the clothing they need.
  How many scholars began to wander about,
    with their bags on their shoulders,
  Despised in the streets, begging the
    strangers, despaired and suffering. [...]
  But also a group of fools among us
    began to behave there like a bunch of wolves,
  Prowling the streets whenever they like
    and stealing whatever they find. [...][25]

This poem clearly reflects the situation of mass exile as described by Austin Jersild: the mountaineers' refusal to work and their total loss of orientation and initiative. The poem also mentions the fate of Muslim scholars in exile: as their profession – leading the congregation, teaching in a *maktab* or *madrasa*, and research – wholly depends on a functioning Muslim community, they found themselves deprived of any possibility to make a living and began to "wander about". This was certainly not the fate of Hasan al-Alqadari who, with the help of some funding from his patron Orbelianov,[26] tried to make the best of his situation: he continued to write poems and *fatwa*s and cultivated his social contacts by mail. Furthermore, he seized the opportunity to visit local Tatar Muslim scholars and discussed ritual and juridical questions with them. Obviously he knew that individual terms of exile usually did not last too long, and sooner or later he would be allowed to return to Daghestan.

Shortly before his death in 1910, al-Alqadari completed another book in Arabic, the *Jirab al-Mamnun* ("Mamnun's Knapsack", Temir-Khan-Shura, 1912).[27] This is a collection of about 150 *fatwa*s that he wrote to more than 30 different addressees who are mostly identified by name. Here again we usually have the texts of both correspondents, i.e., the request (of the *mustafti*) and then al-Alqadari's answer as a *mufti*. Many of these *fatwa*s deal with traditional topics of juridical consultation, namely questions of rites and law. But al-Alqadari also uses the medium of the *fatwa* to touch upon questions of "modern life": for instance, he gives *fatwa*s on the permissibility of using the telegraph[28] and of listening to Qur'an recitations from a gramophone.[29] He even offers consultation on geographical topics like the Wall of Alexander which according to al-Alqadari cannot be identical with the wall near Derbend.[30] Another question of this kind deals with the nature of the Great Ocean (*al-muhit*) which, according to a traditional view, surrounds the whole inhabited world. On this occasion al-Alqadari talks about European inventions and discoveries; for instance, he dwells on America's discovery by Christopher Columbus and that of Oceania by James Cook. Furthermore he teaches that the Earth revolves around the Sun, and he even gives scientific estimations of the Sun's size in comparison to that of the Earth. Reportedly, he obtained these bits of information from an Ottoman textbook on geography which, of course, had European sources. In al-Alqadari's view it is necessary to talk about "the philosophers of our present century", and he claims that it makes no difference whether they are believers (scil. in Islam) or not. Finally he compares the modern geographical and time zones of the Earth with the traditional Islamic concept of "climate zones" (*aqalim*), stating that all these zones are legitimate in their own right because they are based on different definitions for different purposes.[31]

Al-Alqadari's *fatwa*s on traditional questions of *fiqh* mostly deal with topics like the prescribed times for ritual prayers and fasting, subtleties of marriage contracts and questions of inheritance, *waqf* and votive offerings (*nadhr*). Interestingly, several requests were brought forward by people who were themselves in exile, and some of them are directly related to questions of life in a non-Muslim environment. Thus al-Alqadari received a letter from one Ghadanfar Efendi al-Daghistani who was exiled to Irkutsk in Siberia. Ghadanfar asked him about the meaning of the famous *hadith* "He who resembles a group, belongs to it". This is a very delicate *istifta'* which amounts to asking whether wearing Western (Russian) clothing is equivalent to apostasy. Al-Alqadari answers that European clothing as such does not mean unbelief (*kufr*) except if it is explicitly intended to display apostasy.[32] Ghadanfar from Irkutsk also asks him whether a Muslim has the duty to leave non-Muslim territory. This was an urgent question in Daghestan after the end of the *jihad* and also after the 1877 rebellion; for instance, the famous Khalidiyya *shaykh* 'Abd al-Rahman al-Thughuri from Sogratl' in Avaria had written a treatise on this topic, claiming that emigration (*hijra*) was incumbent on every Muslim to enable him to continue *jihad* from his place of exile, which seems to refer to the Ottoman Empire.[33] By contrast, al-Alqadari does not vote for the necessity of *hijra* and *jihad*; according to him, *hijra* is only incumbent when the circumstances of non-

Muslim government do not allow Muslims to perform their religious rituals any more – and it goes without saying that this was not the case in al-Alqadari's contemporary Russia.[34] In another *fatwa*, al-Alqadari deals with the problem whether *zakat* tax has to be taken from the possessions and income of somebody who has been exiled,[35] thus touching upon the impact of exile on the financial and economic situation of the Daghestani community. We can assume that Daghestani villages suffered a great loss of taxes when some of their wealthiest and most influential members were subjected to banishment.

Where attitudes of Sunnis towards other religious groups are concerned, the author always favours what one may label a liberal view. This concerns above all the Shi'is who, according to al-Alqadari, belong to the people of the *qibla* and may not be called Unbelievers.[36] It also concerns social and economic intercourse with non-Muslims; this can be seen from his *fatwa*s on the consumption of meat that has been slaughtered by Christians[37] and on the marriage of *kitabi* women (that is, of Christian or Jewish faith),[38] all of which al-Alqadari declares generally licit. Yet, as so often, this theoretical tolerance ends when it touches closer to home: this happened in Dhu al-Qa'da 1312/April-May 1895 when one of al-Alqadari's sons wished to marry a girl of Lutheran faith, a certain 'Yelena bint Vladimir' from St. Petersburg. Hasan al-Alqadari wrote a short poem to dissuade his son from this marriage. The poem failed of its desired effect.[39]

Although al-Alqadari, like most of his Daghestani correspondents and readers, belonged to the Shafi'i *madhhab*, in many of his answers he cites Hanafi sources as well, thus stating two points of view in the Islamic genre of *ikhtilaf*. Dissent between Hanafis and Shafi'is appears, for example, on the question whether it is permissible to eat horse meat.[40] Practical problems are also dealt with in a *fatwa* on the question how to proceed when the imam of a mosque is a Hanafi but its preacher (*khatib*) is a Shafi'i.[41] In several cases al-Alqadari seems to be inclined to the Hanafi argument; in one instance, he polemicizes against partisanship (*ta'assub*) for only one school of law and quotes the famous Egyptian (Shafi'i) scholar al-Suyuti (d. 1505) to the effect that Islamic law cannot forbid a change of *madhhab*.[42]

In one answer from 1297/1879-80 written in Spassk, al-Alqadari states clearly that in his place of exile he had only a limited number of Shafi'i law books at his disposal.[43] It seems likely, therefore, that al-Alqadari's sojourn in a Hanafi milieu was one reason why he quoted at length from Hanafi books which, presumably, he borrowed from Tatar *mullah*s in the vicinity. Thus we can say that it was the special situation of exile which forced our Shafi'i

jurisconsult to deal intensively with Hanafi discussions and to reflect on the differences between the two *madhhab*s. As far as I can see, al-Alqadari's *Jirab al-Mamnun* is the first text of
this kind written by a Daghestani *'alim*. Just as in other Muslim countries at the same time
or slightly later, so here we find a development towards a new and perhaps more critical relation to one's own legal school, a relationship less permeated by a sense of partisanship.

All in all, it seems to me that al-Alqadari's works on law and poetry are traditional only in
form; they are much less so in content. The function of his two books in particular is quite
original, for we can say that al-Alqadari's poetical *Diwan* and his *fatwa*-compilation taken
together make up his very personal autobiography. Seen from this angle, the poetry reveals
the author's inner, emotional side and his personal relations to friends and teachers, while
the *fatwa*s account for his outward, professional activities. Also, we have seen that al-Alqadari uses traditional forms of scholarly discourse to convey modern European knowledge to
his countrymen. I dare say that his writings had more appeal to the Muslims in the Daghestani mountains than, for example, the efforts of the so-called "modernist" educational re-
formers in Temir-Khan-Shura and Petrovsk (nowadays Makhachkala), who in the eyes of
traditional Muslims just copied Russian educational methods and contents and thus turned
away from the path of Islam.

III

Our examples show that in the second half of the 19th century and until the Russian revolution, Daghestani Muslim culture entered a process of re-opening and widening of its ho-
rizon. When the *jihad* and the Russian blockade came to an end, new contacts with Muslims outside the northern Caucasus became possible. Among the first Daghestanis to establish such contacts were those *shaykh*s, scholars, *qadi*s and officers who for one reason or another were sent into exile to Inner Russia. Although exile was instituted as a political and
administrative means to isolate Muslims from their home communities and to destroy old
networks, it also stimulated new contacts with other Muslims. This led to the transformation of Sufi groups and to scholarly communication beyond the boundaries of the individual's own legal school.

As for the *shaykh*s Mahmud al-Almali and Sayfallah al-Nitsubkri, their banishment enabled them to make new Sufi acquaintances and thus to expand their own *tariqa* networks into other regions, especially into the Middle and Lower Volga. At the same time, the new acquaintances influenced the Sufi discourse in Daghestan, for they gave birth to new *tariqa* branches that explicitly abstained from *jihad*. Obviously, the *shaykh*s profited from the *Pax Russica* and the Empire's communications facilities. Yet in general the Sufis did not reflect on Russia in terms of culture, as a different civilization they had to cope with; rather, they continued to confine themselves to their classical Sufi discourse with but slight variations on the main questions of Sufi ritual.

Hasan al-Alqadari goes a step further. As an officer in Russian service he not only recognizes the futility of any political or military opposition to the Empire but also acknowledges that Russia's Muslims have to gain some access to Europe's technical and scientific progress. In spite of his own temporary misfortune at the hands of the Russian regime, al-Alqadari continues to plead for the Daghestanis' integration into Russian modernity. Yet also for him this does not mean giving up traditional Muslim identity. According to al-Alqadari, the schools of Islamic law provide enough flexible provisions to adapt to new circumstances, and they allow for certain types of social intercourse with non-Muslim communities in a country that is governed by Christians.

These few examples show that the complex of exile is much more ambiguous than one might have expected. First, we have to draw a line between mass exile and individual banishment. Secondly, we find that individual exile was not only applied to notorious enemies of the State but – perhaps more often – to persons like the *qadi* and *shaykh* Sayfallah al-Nitsubkri and the officer and *faqih* Hasan al-Alqadari who, as far as we can tell, were quite loyal servants to the Russian administration of Daghestan but fell into disgrace for reasons not entirely known to us. Thus the mere fact that a Muslim figure was sent into exile does not necessarily tell us much about his convictions and activities.

And thirdly, exile produced a huge amount of literature that still has to be explored. At a time when a considerable part of the intellectual elite of Daghestan was in exile, Sufi correspondence as well as poems and *fatwa*s sent out to friends in Astrakhan, Riazan, Troitsk, Saratov and even Siberia fulfilled an important function: they kept people connected and maintained a discourse. We should keep in mind that until 1905 there were almost no Muslim newspapers in circulation, and all communication between exiles and their home country depended on personal ties and correspondence. But as most of the exiles returned to the northern Caucasus after a certain time, their experience in Russia directly affected Daghestani culture at home – maybe even in a more lasting way than the experience of those Daghestanis who chose to emigrate to the Ottoman Empire and to stay there for ever.

NOTES

1   On blood revenge and its variations see for instance Maksim Kovalevskii, *Zakon i Obychai na Kavkaze*, Vol. II (Moscow 1890), pp. 222ff.
2   Austin Jersild, 'Imperial Russification: Daghestani Mountaineers in Russian Exile, 1877–83', *Central Asian Survey* Vol. 19, No. 1 (2000), pp. 5-16.
3   Natal'ya Tagirova and Amri R. Šixsaidov, "Abdarrahman al-Gazigumuqi und seine Werke', in Michael Kemper, Anke von Kügelgen and Dmitriy Yermakov (eds.), *Muslim Culture in Russia and Central Asia from the 18th to the Early 20th Centuries*, Vol. 1 (Berlin 1996), p. 323. Abdurrakhman al-Gazigumuki, *Kratkoe izlozhenie podrobnogo opisaniia del imama Shamilia (Khulasat al-Tafsil)* transl. and ed. Natal'ia Tagirova (Moscow, 2002).
4   Moshe Gammer, 'The Beginnings of the Naqshbandiyya in Daghestan and the Russian Conquest of the Caucasus', *Die Welt des Islams*, 34 (1994), pp. 204-17. For the political and military history of the *jihad* see id., *Muslim Resistance to the Tsar: Shamil and the Conquest of Chechnia and Daghestan*, London 1994; Michael Kemper, *Herrschaft, Recht und Islam in Daghestan. Von den Khanaten und Gemeindbünden zum ihad-Staat* (Wiesbaden, 2005).
5   See M.A. Abdullaev, *Deiatel'nost' i vozzreniia sheikha Abdurakhmana-Khadzhi i ego rodosloviia* (Makhachkala 1998), p. 98, and Nadhir al-Durgili (1891–1935), *Nuzhat al-Adhhan fi Tarajim 'Ulama' Daghistan*, ed. and transl. by Michael Kemper and Amri R. Shikhsaidov, *Muslim Culture in Russia and Central Asia, vol. 4: Die Islamgelehrten Daghestans und ihre Werke* (Berlin, 2004), pp. 234-236. According to Abdullaev, Ilyas al-Tsudaqari lived in exile until 1889.
6   Al-Durgili, *op. cit.*, pp. 234-236; Allen J. Frank, *Muslim Religious Institutions in Imperial Russia. The Islamic World of Novouzensk District and the Kazakh Inner Horde, 1780–1910* (Leiden, 2001), pp. 156-7; id., 'The History of Alti Ata by Muhammad-Fatih and Muhammad al-Ilmini (Introduction, Turkic Text and Translation)', in Anke von Kügelgen, Aširbek Muminov and Michael Kemper (eds.), *Muslim Culture in Russia and Central Asia*, Vol. 3: *Arabic, Persian and Turkic Manuscripts* (Berlin, 2000), p. 434.
7   Ilyas al-Tsudaqari al-Sakin fi Baldat Nawu Uzinski, *Sullam al-Murid* (Kazan, 1904).
8   On Shaykh Mahmud and the Khalidiyya-Mahmudiyya branch, cf. Michael Kemper, 'Khalidiyya Networks in Daghestan and the Question of Jihad (19th – Early 20th Centuries)', *Die Welt des Islams*, Vol. 42, No. 1 (2002), pp. 41-71.
9   According to the Tatar *shaykh* and biographer Muhammad Murad al-Ramzi (al-Manzilawi, d. 1934), Mahmud was exiled to Perm province 'because he fell suspect to the Government', and after being released he visited Kazan before going to Astrakhan – *Talfiq al-Akhbar wa-Talqih al-Athar fi Waqa'i' Qazan wa-Bulghar wa-Muluk al-Tatar*, Vol. II (Orenburg, 1908), p. 475.
10 This was a certain Shaykh Hashim al-Yamashani; see Shu'ayb b. Idris al-Bagini, *Tabaqat al-Khwajagan al-Naqshbandiyya wa-Sadat al-Mashayikh al-Khalidiyya al-Mahmudiyya*, ed. 'Abd al-Jalal al-'Ata (Damascus 1317 [1899-1900]), p. 446. It seems that al-Yamashani also stemmed from the Southern Caucasus, since there are *silsilas* connecting him directly with Isma'il al-Kurdamiri-al-Shirwani – Mir Khalid Sayfallah b. Husayn Bashlar al-Nitsubkri al-Ghazi-Ghumuqi al-Naqshbandi al-Qadiri al-Shadhili al-Shafi'i al-Daghistani, *Maktubat Khalid Sayfallah ila Fuqara Ahl Allah* (Damascus, 1998), letter 6.
11 Al-Bagini, *op. cit.*, p. 469.
12 Al-Ramzi, *op. cit.*, Vol. II, p. 484.
13 For the interesting biography of Sayfallah Qadi al-Nitsubkri Bashlarov as a Sufi, *mufti*, politician and medical man see now Shamil' Shikhaliev's entry "Saypulla-kadi" in S.M. Prozorov (ed.), *Islam na territorii byvshei Rossiiskoi Imperii. Entsiklopedicheskii slovar'*, vypusk IV, (Moscow, 2003), pp. 72-73.
14 *Maktubat Khalid Sayfallah*, letter 20.
15 Ibid., letter 34.
16 Ibid., letters 51, 53, 55, 65.
17 Ibid., letter 32. For the Shadhiliyya see P. Lory, "Shadhiliyya", *EI2*, Vol. IX, pp. 172b – 175a.

18   *Maktubat Khalid Sayfallah*, letter 36.

19   For the Qadiriyya, see Moshe Gammer's contribution in this volume.

20   Al-Alqadari published his autobiography in *Diwan al-Mamnun* (Temir-Khan-Shura, 1913) pp. 1-10; for his exile and the events leading to it, see ibid., pp. 115-81. For a short sketch of al-Alqadari's life and work see Amri R. Shikhsaidov's entry 'al-Alkadari Khasan-Efendi', in S.M. Prozorov (ed.), *Islam na territorii byvshei Rossiiskoi Imperii. Entsiklopedicheskii slovar'*, vypusk II, (Moscow, 1999), pp. 8-9. On different aspects of al-Alqadari's work cf. *Istoriko-literaturnoe nasledie Gasana Alkadari*, (Makhachkala 1988), as well as Sonia Chesnin's contribution in this volume.

21   *Athar-i Daghistan* (St. Petersburg, 1903).

22   On this work, see Sonia G. Ibragimova, 'Zhanrovoe mnogoobrazie "Divana al-Mamnun" Gasana Alkadari', in: *Istoriko-literaturnoe nasledie Gasana Alkadari*, pp. 83-99.

23   Cf. I. Krachkovskii, *Izbrannye sochineniia*, vol. 6 (Moscow-Leningrad, 1960), p. 618.

24   Al-Alqadari's poems show that he made friends with al-Hajj Fakhr al-Din 'Urmanchiev' b. Mulla Murtada who worked as *imam* in the village of Pushal al-Kubra/Pashli al-Kabira (district of Temnikov, province of Tambov; cf. *Diwan*, p. 155). On the occasion of the New Year in 1300/1882, al-Alqadari found himself reciting elegies at the party of a certain *kniaz'* 'Abd al-Hakim, obviously a member of the Tatar nobility in Russian service (ibid., pp. 168-9).

25   Ibid., pp. 167-8. Cf. Durgeli, *op. cit.*, pp. 220-223.

26   Al-Alqadari, *Diwan al-Mamnun*, p. 174.

27   The last date mentioned in the *Diwan* is 1327/1909; the last date mentioned in the *Jirab* is Dhu al-Hijja 1328/December 1910.

28   Al-Alqadari, *Jirab al-Mamnun*, p. 181.

29   Ibid., 243 (to his son Mulla Pasha, Dhu al-Qa'da 1317/March 1900).

30   Ibid., pp. 34-9 (to one Mulla Hajj Karim al-Akhti from southern Daghestan, written in Rabi' I 1293/ March-April 1873).

31   Ibid., pp. 27-34.

32   Ibid., p. 64. Interestingly, Ghadanfar seems to have organized some kind of Muslim instruction in a mosque in Irkutsk, for several of his questions deal with problems of teaching: thus he asks whether the Qur'an may be taught by someone who has no permission from a *murshid*, whether a teacher may look at the girls he teaches, or whether a mosque may be installed in a place where wine had been sold before. Al-Alqadari entitled his 25 *fatwas* to Ghadanfar *Juhd al-Gharib fi Jawab al-Arib* (*Jirab al-Mamnun*, pp. 55-81).

33   *Risala Sharifa lil-Shaykh al-Fadil al-Hajj 'Abd al-Rahman al-Thughuri*, Ms. Princeton, Yahuda Collection, 2867, fols. 91a-94a. It is not entirely clear when this treatise was written. We know that another work on *hijra* was produced when Shamil was still flourishing; its author, the *faqih* Murtada-'Ali al-'Uradi (d. ca. 1865), demanded that in order to carry out *jihad*, every Muslim living in Russian-controlled territories had to emigrate not abroad, but into the lands of Shamil's government. On al-'Uradi, see Michael Kemper, 'The Daghestani Legal Discourse on the Imamate', in *Central Asian Survey* (2002), 21 (3), pp. 269-275.

34   Al-Alqadari, *Jirab al-Mamnun*, pp. 66-7.

35   Ibid., p. 68.

36   Ibid., pp. 61f. It seems that al-Alqadari wrote two separate works in defence of the Shi'a. These are: *Tahqiq al-maqal fi fada'il al-Al*, and *Izhar al hal fi khusus al-Al*; see A.R. Shikhsaidov, 'Rukopisnoe nasledie Alkadari', in *Istoriko-literaturnoe nasledie Gasana Alkadari*, p. 60.

37   Ibid., pp. 45-7.

38   Ibid., pp. 290f. On these disputes in a Hanafi milieu cf. Michael Kemper, *Sufis und Gelehrte in Tatarien und Baschkirien. Der islamische Diskurs unter russischer Herrschaft* (Berlin 1998), pp. 290-9.

39   Al-Alqadari, *Diwan al-Mamnun*, p. 210. The son in question was probably Abu Muslim who was serving in the Tsar's Guards in St. Petersburg; cf. ibid., p. 135.

40   Al-Alqadari, *Jirab al-Mamnun*, p. 47.

41   Ibid., pp. 78-9.

42   Ibid., pp. 50-1. Another question (presented, by the way, by Shaykh Shu'ayb al-Bagini, the important Sufi biographer of the Khalidiyya-Mahmudiyya branch whose *Tabaqat* have been quoted above) was whether a Hanafi Muslim who married a Shafi'i woman has to renew his act of marriage when he changes over to the Shafi'i school (ibid., p. 158). Al-Alqadari cites several sources to the effect that the old marriage is valid.

43   Ibid., p. 54

A DARGHI CODEX OF CUSTOMARY LAW AND ITS CONTRIBUTION TO LINGUISTICS

HELMA VAN DEN BERG

INTRODUCTION

In this article I shall explore one particular manuscript written in the Darghi language,[1] dating back to the seventeenth century. This manuscript contains a codex of customary law from the Kaytag-Darghi area. The text of this manuscript was documented, analyzed, translated and published in 1964 by Professor Rasul Magomedov in Makhachkala. The text on which his work and my research are based is a copy from 1828 made by qadi Nuh in the village of Kishcha. This copy is apparently kept nowadays in Makhachkala.

It was, and still is, generally believed that we do not have written historical documents in the Daghestani languages which provide us with information about the history and development of the languages in that region, supposedly because these languages received their writing systems and their speakers became literate only after the 1917 revolution. True as this might be from a general point of view, it is clear that there do exist earlier documents, written in some of the local Daghestani languages, in the Arabic script. Apart from the historical value that they have, these may well also be of interest to linguists. In my opinion, the study of this and other early Darghi documents adds an extra dimension to the typological and historical comparison of Darghi dialects. The study of Darghi dialects is necessary in order to reconstruct earlier stages of the Darghi language; usually in comparative historical research early written documents are taken into account as well, but this has never been done before for Daghestani languages.

In this article I present the preliminary results of the study of this document from a linguistic point of view. In the future I should like to be able to locate the original manuscript in Daghestan and produce a new annotated edition of the text, which would deal with linguistic issues. In doing so, it will be clear that we need to find, catalogue and study more documents of this type, in order to be able to shed light on the historical development of Darghi and other Daghestani languages.

THE DARGHI CODEX: BACKGROUND

The Darghi codex consists of 29 pages of Darghi text in Arabic script, with seven or eight lines to the page. There are one or more lacunae in the text where leaves from the manuscript have been lost. The text is divided into subsections, separated by the words muħli bucalli, bek' bucar 'if you guard your mouth, your head will be safe'. Fragment (1) is the transliteration[2] and analysis[3] of the first page of the text.

(1) Opening fragment:
1.1.
bi-smi   l-lāhi   r-raħmāni   r-raħīm
'In the name of God, the Beneficent, the Merciful'
1.2.
hayš xaydaq darkah   ziǧ-n-a-lla   kka   sa<b>i
this   Kaytag   Dargo responsibility-PL-OBL-GEN   codexbe:N
'this is the behavioural code of Kaytag Dargo'
1.3.
li<b>il   uccumm-a-la   darkka   barxbalkuyy b-alk-un-il
all:N ucmi-OBL-GEN Dargo consent   N-write-AOR-ADJ
'with the consent of whole Ucmi-Dargi it was written'
1.4.
sa<b>i   kkiša-la   ši-li-zzi   ka<b>ix^-ib-il   sa<b>i/
be:N Kishcha-GEN   village-OBL-ILL put:N-AOR-ADJ be:N
b-učč=an-i-s
N-read=AG-OBL-DAT
'it was put down in the village of Kishcha; to the reader'

1.5.

daray /	ya+ħabal	qur	talqay-s	unc/
silk	or+three rouble		ruler-DAT	ox

'silk or three roubles, for the ruler an ox'

1.6.

talqa nuhru akka-li ma-b-ilč-ab / b-ilč-ali

ruler:GEN seal absent-ADV PROH-N-read-OPT3 N-read-COND3

talqay-s#

ruler:OBL-DAT

'without the seal of the ruler, let it not be read, if it is read, to the ruler'

1.7.

urči / talqay b-ilčč=iq-al# určči b-ik-ab

horse ruler:ERG N-read=CAUS-COND3 horse N-give-OPT3

b-ilčč-un-il-i

N-read-AOR-ADJ-OBL

'a horse; if the ruler makes it read, let a horse be given to the reader'

2.1.

muħli	b-ucc-ali	bik	b-ucc-ar...
mouth	N-guard-COND3	head	N-guard-FUT3

'if the mouth is safeguarded, the head will be safe...'

According to Magomedov[4] the language of this codex is the Urkarakh-Kaytag dialect. This presents our first problem. First of all, most of our knowledge of Darghi and its various dialects concerns the standard written language (darginskii literaturnyi iazyk), one of the main dialects (Akusha, Urakhi), or a more remote dialect (Kubachi, Megeb, Chirag, Itsari). The other Darghi dialects have not been studied in detail. Thus linguists who are not native Darghi speakers simply do not know what the characteristics of the Urkarakh and Kaytag dialects are.

The second problem in this regard is that preliminary historical research by Starostin and Testelec, as given in Table 1, shows that Urkarakh and Kaytag belong to quite different branches of Darghi; these diverged from each other at a fairly early stage. If the manuscript shows features from both dialects, this could perhaps be due to the copying. Qadi Nuh lived in Kishcha, the Urkarakh area.

South Darghi	Itsari-Sirkha	Itsari	
		Sirkha	
	Kaytag		
	Megeb		
Proto-Darghi	North Darghi	Central Darghi	Mugi-Akusha
			Muiri (Urkarakh)
			Tsudakhar
			Gubden
			V.Mulebki-Urakhi
	Chirag-Kubachi		

Table 1: Dialects in historical perspective (Starostin and Testelec, op. cit.)

Magomedov[5] gives an introduction to the history of the Kaytag area followed by a discussion of the manuscript in its historical context, which I summarize here. The formation of Kaytag-Dargo goes back to the period of the Arab conquest of the East Caucasus. After the conquest, the Arabs themselves did not start to live among the population they had just conquered, but appointed rulers from the local ruling class; the name used for that type of ruler is ucmi. Instead of the term Kaytag-Dargo we also find Ucmi-Dargo, which underlines the rule of the ucmi in this part of Daghestan.

The background for the creation of this codex must have been the wish to strengthen rule in Kaytag-Dargo. The population of Kaytag-Dargo belonged to different ethnic groups and social layers. The main power of the Kaytag rulers was in Lower Kaytag, where the rulers managed to subdue the rural population. In Upper Kaytag, however, the village communities kept their internal structure and their rights to the land. This restricted the influence of the ucmi to a large extent. After a period of violent but indecisive clashes between the ucmi and the independent communities, they agreed to settle some common rules, which are reflected in this Darghi codex, composed during the rule of Rustam-Khan (1601–45).

The main task of the ucmi was to protect Kaytag-Dargo from intrusion from outside and to lead military actions against external enemies, but not without consulting the (Upper Kaytag) local councils (3).

(3)

25.7.

talqay   ʕaqlu-la b-ah-t-a-ci   kkinkkiš akka-li   ħuriba
ruler:ERG mind-GEN hpl-head-PL-OBL-ILL? absent-ADV swarm
'the ruler without the advice of the elders a swarm'

26.1.

ddura+ma-ʔ-ab   b-ukk-al#   ħabc#li / t mān   ʕakka   b-ih-ab
out+PROH-be-OPT3 N-lead-COND3 thirty tuman penalty N-be-OPT3
'let him not take up; if he leads it, let there be a penalty of 30 tuman'

26.2.

kkinkkiš+b-arq-ib-li /   ca   abirx-ulli /   ħa-b-uqq-ali
ʔ+N-act-AOR-GER   one   ʔ-GER   NEG-N-leave-COND3
'after consultation, if they do not go out as one'

26.3.

bik+bik-la   daršal   tankka ʕakka   b-ih-ab/...
head+head-GEN hundred measure penalty N-be-OPT3
'let there be a penalty of hundred measures from each'

Another task of the ucmi was to maintain law and to pronounce verdicts in case of juridical disputes. The codex contains both civil and criminal law, and thus provides us with a number of regulations and rules designed as a guide to behaviour in the community of Kaytag-Dargo. Various types of crime are described and discussed, with their proper punishment. (examples 4, 5).

(4)

9.7.

… adim-t-a-la   qawǧa+d-ih-ub-li ca-li+ca b-aqq-alli

person-PL-OBL-GEN fight+pl-be-AOR-GER one-OBL:ERG+one N-hit-COND3

'if in a fight of people the one hits the other'

10.1.

[…]lli   w-ibkk-ib-il-i-s / ʕilli   w-ibkk-ib-il-li

ʔM-die-AOR-ADJ-OBL-DAT   after   M-die-AOR-ADJ-OBL:ERG

buq-ra   lukk-is-li 10.2   b-ih-ab…

penalty-AND   give-INF-GER   N-be-OPT3

'let the one who dies later give a penalty to the one who dies first'

(5)

3.5.

……ka<w>š-alli   wirħdaħ

kill:M-COND3   sevenfold   'if someone is killed, sevenfold'

3.6.

ħi+d-ih-ab /   anruka ka<w>š-ali   ara-li   uk-uħili

blood+pl-be-OPT3 robber kill:M-COND3 robbery-OBL M:spend-WHEN

'let there be blood(feud); if a robber is killed during a robbery'

3.7.

tak+ih-ab /   ǧanruka ka<w>š-ib-il   ka<w>š-alli /   hal   musa-li-ki-b

ʔ+M:be-OPT3   robber   kill:M-AOR-ADJ kill:M-COND3 this   p l a c e - O B L -
SUP-N

'let it be; if the killer of a robber is killed on the spot'

3.8

čidaħ   ħi+d-ah-ab…

twice   blood+pl-be-OPT3   'let there be blood twice'

The codex reflects a number of features of Daghestani customary law, e.g., blood feud (see example (5)), hospitality extended to enemies as well (6), kidnapping of the bride (7), common responsibility of relatives (8).

(6)

10.6.

...dušm   w-akk-ali   w-iħ-as-li

enemy   M-come-COND3M-keep-INF-GER

'if an enemy comes'

10.7.

b-ah-ab /   ma-w-udda   ħ(a/i)-yk-is-li   b-ah-ab/

N-be-OPT3   PROH-M-be-FUT2 NEG-M:say-INF-GER N-be-OPT3

'let him be received, don't say 'you can't stay''

11.1.

arq-āli   w-arx   ħa-wq-as-li+b-ah-ab/...

leave-COND3   M-with   NEG-M:leave-INF-GER+N-be-OPT3

'if he leaves, don't leave together with him'

(7)

7.5.

......amarsa-li   x^unul

?-OBL:ERG   woman

'a man(?) a woman'

7.6.

ha<r>as-ali /   ha<r>as-ib-il-i-ki   rāzi+r-ih-alli

take.away:F-COND3   take-AOR-ADJ-OBL-SUP glad+F-be-COND3

'if he leads her away, and if she agrees to her being led away'

7.7.

r-ikk-is-li   b-ah-ab   rāzi+ħa-r-ih-ali   b-aʕ-ti-ra+ki-r

F-give-INF-GER N-be-OPT   glad+NEG-F-be-COND3 hpl-head-PL-AND+SUP-F

'let her be given away, if she does not agree and if her parents'

7.8.

kk-ā   b-ikk-ālli   ki<r>ikk-is-li   b-ah-ab……

give.back:F-IMP hpl-say-COND3 give:F-INF-GER N-be-OPT3

'say 'give her back', let him give her back'

(8)

20.6.

adimi   wahi /   irx-ulli / tuxum-li   ka<w>š-is-li

person   bad   ?-GER   tukhum-OBL:ERG   kill:M-INF-GER

'if a man behaves badly, let the tukhum kill him,'

20.7.

b-ih-ab /   ka<ta><w>š-alli   č"u-li   aqq-is-li b-ih-ab

N-be-OPT3   kill:?:M-COND self:PL:OBL-? ?-INF-GER   N-be-OPT3

'if they do not kill him, then they should hold him responsible'

Law was maintained by the local council (jamaʿat). The punishment for those not adhering to the common rules of customary law was the destruction of their houses and exile (9).

(9)

23.4.

ca   šan-ti-wan /   ǧ ay   b-ikk-is-li   b-ih-ab

one   village-PL-ID   word   hpl-say-INF-GER N-be-OPT3

'let the villagers speak as one'

23.5.

dikkar uqq-un-il-la   qqali   b-uʔ-is-li

different M:leave-AOR-ADJ-GEN house   N-destroy-INF-GER

b-ih-ab / sa.y-ra

N-be-OPT3   self:M-AND

'let the house of the one who breaks away be destroyed and himself'

23.6.

ddura+w-irkk-is-li b-ih-ab

     out+M-ʔ-INF-GER   N-be-OPT3   'be exiled'

DARGHI MANUSCRIPTS IN ARABIC SCRIPT

Isaev[6] gives an overview of printed documents in Arabic script in Avar, Darghi, Kumyk, Lak and some other Caucasian languages; no publications in Lezgi are mentioned. The number of publications varies considerably from language to language, 152 pieces for Kumyk, 90 pieces for Avar; Darghi and Lak have 34 pieces each. The overview is based on chronicles, sales brochures (Mavrayev's Fihrist al-kutub) and Isayev's own findings in Moscow, Petersburg and private libraries in Daghestan. This overview contains printed matter only. A catalogue of manuscripts written in Daghestani languages in Arabic script still needs to be compiled.

Daghestani orientalists have concentrated mainly on the study of manuscripts in Arabic; the fact that the Arabic script has also been used to write the local Daghestani languages has not always been acknowledged. A detailed overview of the manuscripts and archives in Arabic found in Dagestan is given in Gamzatov.[7] A catalogue of Arabic manuscripts was edited by Saidov.[8] Moreover, due to the political circumstances, the existence of these manuscripts could not be discussed for a long time, for they represented the ideology and culture of Islam.

> Due to this and a series of other reasons and factors, a lot of scholars and socio-cultural workers in one way or another deny the presence of literacy and of a written literature among the peoples of pre-revolutionary Daghestan; by doing so, they unjustifiably present the social-political and ethical lifestyle of these peoples as archaic and deny their cultural inheritance.[9]

Opinions vary about the earliest document containing Darghi words. According to Saidov[10] the first such document is a manuscript of Ihya' 'Ulum al-Din, by Abu Hamid al-Ghazali, copied in 1501[11] by Idris b. Ahmad al-Aqushi. In the margins of this manuscript 29 Darghi words or phrases are found. Isaev[12] mentions this document as well, but adds two earlier ones: Kitab al-Kifaya by Salih b. Anas al-Khashnawi, copied by Muhammad b. Abi Khalid in 1243, with some 200 Darghi words; and Minhaj al-'Abidin by al-Ghazali, copied in 1493[13] by the same Idris b. Ahmad al-Aqushi; this manuscript apparently contains a larger number of Darghi words, as comments to the Arabic text.

This shows us that long before the twentieth century the Darghi people wrote their native language. In the eighteenth and nineteenth centuries enough people in Daghestan knew Arabic to produce a Daghestani literature in Arabic: literature flourished in these centuries and works were produced in a great number of fields, including linguistics, history, philosophy, ethics, logic, law, medicine, astronomy and mathematics. At the same time, personal correspondence, wills and testaments, and poetry were written in the local languages.

ARABIC SCRIPT USED FOR DAGHESTANI LANGUAGES

Even the first writer of Darghi phrases, Idris b. Ahmad, already adapted the Arabic script. The Arabic alphabet has 28 letters, whereas Darghi has about 35 phonemes (in the Akusha dialect; other dialects may have more or fewer). The adapted script, the 'ajam, makes use of diacritics, and thus contains 32 letters: one grapheme represents more than one phoneme.[14] The Akusha-Darghi phonological system is given in table 2, the 'ajam system for the codex in table 3.

Obstruents	plosive			affricate			fricative	
	vcd	asp	ej	vcd	asp	ej	vcd	vcl
labial	b	p	p'					
alveolar	d	t	t'	dz	c	c'	z	s
palatal				dž	č	č'	ž	š
velar	g	k	k'				ĝ	x^
uvular	G	q	q'					x
pharyngeal	ʕ							ħ
glottal			ʔ					h

Resonants: m, n, l, r, w, y.

Vowels: i, e, ä, a, u.

Table 2: Akusha-Darghi phoneme inventory

Arabic sign	Darghi phoneme
أ	a (ā)
ب	b
ت	t
ث	occurs only in *mathala* (7.3.,16.2.) 'for instance'
ج	occurs only in *masjid* (12.7.) 'mosque'
ح	ħ
خ	x
د	d
ذ	does not occur in codex
ر	r
ز	z
س	s
ش	š
ص	occurs only in: *ṣay-či-b-il-la* (18.6.) (< *šay* < *šali* 'side')
ض	occurs only in: *qāḍi* (11.7.) 'qadi', *ramaḍān* (12.5.) 'Ramaḍan'
ط	occurs in: *ṭamna-li* (5.4.) 'with noise', *kaṭṭi* (8.4.), *kkaṭṭi* (9.1.), *xaṭā* (13.7.), *xaṭā-li* (14.4.) 'fault?', *čuhuṭ* (16.1.) 'Jew'
ظ	occurs only in: *ẓulmu* (23.2.) 'force', *ẓalim-t-a-s* (23.6.) 'to the oppressors', *ẓālim-ta-ʕilli* (23.7.) 'oppressors'

Arabic sign	Darghi phoneme
ع	ʕ
غ	
ف	p (f)
ق	q
ك	k
ل	l
م	m
ن	n
ه	h
و	w (ū)
ي	y (ī)
ء	ʔ
◌َ	a, e
◌ِ	i, e
◌ُ	u
	c
	č
	x^
	x^

Table 3: ʿAjam system in the codex

According to Isaev,[15] the Arabic alphabet may not be the optimum choice as the basis for phonemic orthographies for the Daghestani languages, but the 'ajam played a positive role in the situation of multi-dialectality. A written standard did not exist and authors wrote in their own dialects. The use and development of the 'ajam was spontaneous and unplanned. Before the Russian Revolution no standard written language had been developed for any of the Daghestani languages.

After the revolution, the traditional Arabic alphabet was reformed: the vowels were included in-line, no longer as diacritics. The political opinion that

> this alphabet, onto which everything old, outlived hangs, needs to be thrown away and replaced with a new, rational alphabet[16]

resulted in the introduction of the Latin alphabet in 1928 and later, in 1938, in the introduction of the Cyrillic alphabet. A short attempt at the beginning of the twentieth century to use Uslar's alphabet was not successful.

The discussion in most of the literature has been over the questions, first, whether or not the Arabic script represents a suitable tool for writing the Daghestani languages, and second, whether literacy existed among the Daghestani peoples before the Revolution. It should be remembered that this was more a political than a scientific discussion. Without going into this matter too deeply, I tend to agree with Isaev[17] that the use of the Arabic script to represent the Darghi phonological system may have its shortcomings from a linguistic point of view, but this is to a large extent true also for the current Cyrillic script. Here as well, one Darghi phoneme has to be represented by more than one grapheme; the practical use of the alphabet is considered to be difficult; the alphabet needs to be studied, practised and repeated even in the highest grades in school; and writing and reading have to be encouraged in extra-curriculum activities.

With regard to the question of literacy, we have to conclude that the various Daghestani peoples most probably enjoyed restricted literacy at the end of the nineteenth century. The Arabic language provided them with the Arabic script, which served as an entrance into writing the local languages. This was most likely confined to certain professional groups. Nowadays, the situation has improved tremendously: Darghi language education is available at schools in the Darghi districts, though not always in urban schools. Furthermore, Darghi is being taught at institutes of higher education in Makhachkala, Derbend, and Izberbash. Nevertheless, a good many Darghi speakers have difficulty reading their native language, a problem which results from the discrepancy between the written standard and the various dialects. Those members of the cultural élite who have received higher education and use the language professionally, like teachers, journalists, editors, and writers, have a better command of written Darghi.

LINGUISTIC ANALYSIS

The linguistic analysis of the codex has been carried out as follows: the text has been transliterated anew from the copy of the manuscript in Magomedov (1964). There are some divergences between Magomedov's transliteration and mine, which may also be due to mistakes in typesetting. Following this the text was analyzed with interlinear glosses and a lexicon was set up. Data of the Urkarakh and Kishcha dialects were taken from Gasanova[18] though it is generally felt that this publication should be handled with caution. As I had no overview of the dialectal features of Kaytag other than the system of local cases (see 5.2.), the comparison with that dialect largely remains to be done.

Phonology

Double consonants, i.e., consonants written with the sign shadda in Arabic script, may denote ejective consonants, voiced consonants, or neither of them. Usually variants of the same words with a single consonant are also found.

Examples of double consonants denoting ejectives are (with the Standard Darghi form in brackets), e.g.: ʕakka, ʕaka (ʕäk'a) 'penalty', bikk, bik (bek') 'head', dikkar, dikar (dek'ar) 'different', sikkal (sek'al) 'thing', qqabli (q'äbla) 'obligation' -ilč, ilčč (-elč') 'read', -akk, -ak (-ak') 'come', -arqq, -arq (-arq')/-irq, -irqq (-irq') 'do, act'. There are also instances of a single consonant expressing an ejective, without having a variant with a double consonant, e.g: qabul (q'abul) 'agreement', qac (q'ac) 'bread'.

Examples of double consonants denoting voiced consonants are, e.g., akkar, akkal, akkara (agar) 'absent', lukk (lug) 'give' vs. -ilukk (-elk') 'write', darkka, darka, darkah, darkkah, darkkaw (darga) 'Dargo', nikk (neⵣ) 'chaff', -ikk (-ig) 'like' vs. -ikk (-ik') 'say' vs. -ikk (g) 'give', qqana (Gäna) 'lie', qqaǧ (Gaǧ) 'nonsense', naqq (näG) 'hand'.

Double consonants however do not always indicate ejectivity or voice: mulkk, mulk (mulk) 'property', qqali, qali (qali) 'house', určči, urči (urči) 'horse', ulkka (ulka) 'land', daqqi, daqqa (däqi) 'wound', qulki, qulkki, qqulki, qulčči, qulči (qulki) 'thief', -uc, -ucc (-uc) 'safeguard', and also ddura (dura) 'outside', ddapri (dabri) 'shoes', daršal, daššal (daršal) 'hundred'.

In the Kishcha dialect /kk/ is the equivalent of Akusha-Darghi /g/ and this phenomenon is even more widely attested in the Urkarakh dialect, where /pp/ corresponds to /b/, /tt/ to /d/, /ss/ to /s/, /šš/ to /š/. This might explain some of the geminated consonants above that do not denote ejectivity.

Variation between /k/ ~ /č/ and /z/ ~ /c/ is regularly attested in the codex, e.g., in the local cases discussed in 5.2. below, in the examples of qulki, qulkki, qqulki, qulčči, qulči (qulki) 'thief', ciǧa, ziǧa (zeǧa?) 'responsibility, moral', ucdan, uzdaa (uzdan?) 'noble', kayc, kayz (kayz) 'become'. This would also reflect the phonological inventories of the Kishcha and Urkarakh dialects, which have qulči, kaycc, and macca (Standard Darghi maza) 'sheep'.

The Arabic script distinguishes three vowel qualities: /a/, /i/, /u/, whereas the Darghi phonological system has five vowels: /a/, /i/, /u/, /e/, and /ä/. The distinction /a/ ~ /ä/ is not made in the 'ajam, nor was it later in the Latin or the Cyrillic script until the late 1950s. Only nowadays is /ä/ rendered with Cyrillic ia. The distinction is phonological, but to a large extent predictable as well. In the text /e/ is rendered by /i/ or /a/. Examples are, e.g.: -ilč (-elč') 'read', sikkal (sek'al) 'thing', =diš (=deš) 'ABSTR', -hili (-heli) 'WHEN', ʕilli (ʕela) 'after', širi (šeri) 'married', -is (-es) 'INF', li-B (le-B) 'be present'; ħa- (ħe-) 'NEG', wirħal (werħel) 'seven'.

This again probably reflects the Kishcha and Urkarakh inventory as they show /i/ or /a/ for /e/ in these cases: sik'al 'thing', bik' 'head', 'li-B 'be present', ħa-la (ħe-la) 'your', ħa-lukk-a 'will not give it', kkaħal (geħel) 'eight'.

Morphology

Daghestani languages are well known for their intricate local case-systems (see for example the description of the Akusha-Darghi system of local cases in van den Berg).[19] In table 4 the local endings found in the codex are compared with those in the various dialects. The Kaytag data come from Khaidakov.[20] The endings found in the codex show a high degree of similarity to the endings in the Urkarakh and Kishcha dialects.

codex	Urkarakh/Kishcha	Kaytag	Akusha/Standard
superlative *-ki, -kki, -či* 'on'	*-ki*	*-če*	*-či*
directive *-ču* 'towards'	*-ču*	-	-
illative *-ci, -cci, -zzi* 'in'	*-cci*	*-cci*	*-zi*
allative *-ʃi* 'near'	*-ʃi*	-	*-ʃi* (idiomatic)

Table 4: Local cases in the codex and various dialects

With regard to the verb, we can only make some minor remarks. In general, the verbal forms in the codex have the same make-up as nowadays: gender prefix – root – causative suffix – tense marker – person marker. There are perfective and imperfective roots. The affixes for tense and aspect are more or less similar to the current ones. The participial ending -il used in the codex is not used in this function in Akusha and Standard Darghi; there we find -si, but -il is used in quite a number of dialects, including also the Kishcha and Urkarakh dialects. The ending of the infinitive found in the text is -is, which corresponds to Akusha or Standard Darghi -es; however, in the Urkarakh dialect the infinitive ending supposedly is -ana, -ara.[21] Here the parallelism between the codex and the Urkarakh dialect falls short.

Syntax

The main discourse pattern found is 'if X, let it be that Y': the codex contains a large number of conditional forms and optatives, quite a few supines, but fewer verb forms of other types. There is little we can say at this moment about the agreement patterns for gender and person, co-reference in subordination and other phenomena in syntax.

Lexicon

There are quite a few lexemes which I have been unable to trace so far, like (a)marsar 'person?', amxar/amħar 'respectful person'; they may be of Arabic or Persian origin or dialectal. Several Darghi verbs also seem to be used with meanings different from what I have come across so far.

CONCLUSION

The text is fairly easy to read, though there are some parts which are rather difficult to analyse and understand. I hope to be able to clarify these parts in discussion with specialists in Daghestan, and by conducting dialectological research. The main linguistic results seem to be in the field of phonology. In my opinion, the study of the codex in itself is highly interesting from a linguistic point of view, even though only a few linguistic generalizations can be made at this moment.

NOTES

Gratitude is due to Dr. Nico van den Boogert (Leiden), who introduced me to the Arabic script and helped me read the manuscript. I would also like to thank the audience of the 10th Caucasian Colloquium (Munich, August 2000), and the organizers and participants of the conference 'Dagestan in the World of Islam' (Tel Aviv, February 2001) for their interest and useful comments.

1   According to the most recent state of historical comparative research (S.L. Nikolayev and S.A. Starostin, A North Caucasian Etymological Dictionary [Moscow, 1994]), Darghi is a separate branch in the Daghestani subgroup of East Caucasian languages. Other branches are: Avar-Andic, Tsezic, Lak and Lezgic. Currently Darghi is spoken by some 370,000 speakers. Darghi has a written standard, the functioning of which is limited by the broad dialect variety within Darghi.

2   The following special transliteration signs are used: (V) suk n + vowel sign; (a/i) double vocalization; C# consonant without vowel sign or suk n; [...] illegible in the manuscript. / interpunction sign (large inverted comma, single or in cluster of three).

3   The following abbreviations are used: ABSTR abstract, ADJ adjective, ADV adverb, AG agentive, AND coordination particle, AOR aorist, asp aspirated, CAUS causative, COND conditional, DAT dative, ej ejective, ERG ergative, F feminine, GEN genitive, GER gerund, hpl human plural agreement, ID identitive, ILL illative, IMP imperative, INF infinitive, M masculine, N neuter agreement, NEG negative, OBL oblique, OPT optative, pl non-human plural agreement, PL plural suffix, PROH prohibitive, SUP superlative, vcd voiced, WHEN when, 3 third person agreement. A hyphen (-) is used to denote a morpheme boundary; however, the sign = denotes a derivational morpheme boundary, and the sign + denotes a morpheme boundary in compounds; brackets (< and >) are used in the transcription to denote an infix; a colon (:) is used in the glosses to denote the boundary with an infix or a portmanteau morpheme.

4   R.M. Magomedov, Pamiatnik istorii i pis'mennosti dargintsev XVII veka (Makhachkala, 1964), p. 3.

5   Ibid.

6   A.A. Isaev, Katalog pechatnykh knig i publikatsii na iazykakh narodov Dagestana (dorevoliutsionnyi period) (Makhachkala, 1989).

7   G.G. Gamzatov, M.-S. Saidov and A.R. Shikhsaidov, 'Sokrovishchnitsa pamiatnikov pis'mennosti', EIKJa (Tbilisi), IX (1982), pp. 203-23.

8   M.S.D. Saidov (ed.), Katalog arabskikh rukopisei Instituta istorii, iazyka i literatury Dagestanskogo filiala AN SSSR, Vol. 1 (Makhachkala, 1977).

9   A.A. Isaev, 'K voprosu o pis'mennosti narodov Dagestana', Sbornik stat'ei po voprosam dagestanskogo i veinakhskogo iazykoznaniia (Makhachkala, 1972), p. 72.

10 M.S.D. Saidov, 'Iz istorii vozniknoveniia pis'mennosti u narodov Dagestana', Iazyki Dagestana, Vol. III (Makhachkala, 1976), p. 127.

11 Saidov (op. cit., p. 127) and Isaev ('K voprosu', p. 80) date this manuscript to 912/1507, but Gamzatov (op. cit., p. 213) refers to what is apparently the same manuscript with the dating 906/1501.

12 'K voprosu', p. 80.

13 Isaev (ibid., loc. cit.) dates this manuscript to 1493, Gamzatov (op. cit., p. 213) gives 903/1497.

14 Isaev, 'K voprosu', pp. 85-7.

15 Ibid., p. 91.

16   M.M. Gadzhiev, 'Voprosy pis'mennosti dagestanskikh iazykov', Iazyki Dagestana, Vol. II (Makhachkala, 1954), p. 61.
17   Isaev, 'K voprosu', p. 76.
18   S.M. Gasanova, Ocherki darginskoi dialektologii (Makhachkala, 1971).
19   H.E. van den Berg, Dargi folktales. Oral stories from the Caucasus with an introduction to Dargi grammar (Leiden, 2001).
20   S.M. Khaidakov, Darginskii i megebskii iazyki. Printsipy slovoizmeneniia (Moscow, 1985), pp. 35-6.
21   Gasanova, op. cit., pp. 10-11.

ACADEMIA SCIENTIARUM FENNICA HUMANIORA

321. NIKANDER, PIRJO: Age in Action. Membership Work and Stage of Life Categories in Talk. (2002) 242 pp.

322. POE, MARSHALL T.: The Russian Elite in the Seventeenth Century. Volume 1: The consular ranks of the Russian "Sovereign's Court" 1613–1713. (2004) 469 pp.

323. POE, MARSHALL T.: The Russian Elite in the Seventeenth Century. Volume 2: A quantitave analysis of the "Duma Ranks" 1613–1713. (2004) 283 pp.

324. TEUVO LAITILA: The Finnish Guard in the Balkans. Heroism, Imperial loyalty and Finnishness in the Russo-Turkish War of 1877–1878 as recollected in the memoirs of Finnish guardsmen. (2003) 451 pp.

325. Erudition and Eloquence. The use of Latin in the countries of the Baltic Sea (1500–1800). Acts of a Colloquium held in Tartu, 23–26 August, 1999. Edited by OUTI MERISALO and RAIJA SARASTI-WILENIUS. (2003) 242 pp.

326. HEIKKILÄ, TUOMAS: Vita S. Symeonis Treverensis. Ein hochmittelalterlicher Heiligenkult im Kontext. (2002) 330 pp.

327. BARTENS, ANGELA: A Contrastive Grammar Islander – Caribbean Standard English – Spanish. (2003) 175 pp.   .

328. LALLUKKA, SEPPO: From Fugitive Peasants to Diaspora. The Eastern Mari in Tsarist and Federal Russia. (2003) 473 pp.

329. KIISKINEN, TERHI: The Library of the Finnish Nobleman, Royal Secretary and Trustee Henrik Matsson (ca. 1540–1617). (2004) 299 pp.

331. MEOUAK, MOHAMED: Saqâliba, eunuques et esclaves à la conquête du pouvoir. Géographie et histoire des élites politiques «marginales» dans l'Espagne umayyade. (2004) 301 pp.

332. AHVENAINEN, JORMA: The European Cable Companies in South America before the First World War. (2004) 427 pp.

333. HALLENBERG, HELENA: A Saint Invented. Ibrāhīm al Dasūqī (1255–1296). (2005) 293 pp.

334. KIVIHARJU, JUKKA: Colección Diplomática del Hospital de Santa Cristina de Somport I (Años 1078–1304). (2004) 426 pp.

335. Russia Takes Shape. Patterns of integration from the Middle Ages to the present. Edited by BOGATYREV, SERGEI. (2005) 289 pp.

336. Rituals and Relations. Edited by SARI MÄNTYLÄ. (2005) 262 pp.

337. MIKKONEN, TUIJA: Corporate Architecture in Finland in the 1940s and 1950s. (2005) 269 pp.

338. LÄHTEENMÄKI, MARIA: The Peoples of Lapland. Boundary demarcations and interaction in the North Calotte from 1808 to 1889. (2006) 336 pp.

339. KANERVA, LIISA: Between Science and Drawings. Renaissance architects on Vitruviu's educational ideas. (2006) 203 pp.

340. EL HOUR, RACHID, La administración judicial almorávide en al-Andalus. Élites, negociaciones y enfrentamientos. (2006) 336 pp.